Jewish Journeys in Jerusalem

A Tourist's Guide

by

Jay Levinson

915.694

John Jay College of Criminal Justice
City University of New York

First Edition 2010
The Key Publishing House Inc.
Toronto, Canada
Website: www.thekeypublish.com
E-mail: info@thekeypublish.com
ISBN 978-0-9811606-7-2 paperback

Copyediting Jennifer South
Cover design & photos Sheina Carlebach Berkowitz
Typesetting and indexing Velin Saramov
Un-credited photos are © Jay Levinson
Photos credited (Sheina) are taken by Sheina Carlebach Berkowitz
Photos credited with © are courtesy of their corresponding site

Library and Archives Canada Cataloguing in Publication

Levinson, Jay
    Jewish journeys in Jerusalem : a tourist's guide / Jay Levinson. – 1st ed.

Includes index.
ISBN 978-0-9811606-7-2

    1. Jerusalem – Guidebooks. 2. Jerusalem–Description and travel.
I. Title.

DS109.15.L48 2010   915.694'420454   C2009-906433-2

Printed and bound in USA. This book is printed on paper suitable for recycling and made from fully sustained forest sources.

Published in association and a grant from The Key Research Center (www.thekeyresearch.org). The Key promotes freedom of thought and expression and peaceful coexistence among human societies.

Introduction

This guide book is geared for the tourist who is looking for a Jewish experience in Jerusalem. It is not a standard checklist of places to be seen. Yes, it does describe where sites are located and their hours. Yes, it does include several secular sites of general interest. The main purpose of the book is to focus on the Jewish aspects of the city and provide background for a better Jewish understanding.

Churches, mosques, and other non-Jewish sites are not included. Some sites are given negative rating, since they are inappropriate for a genuine Jewish experience. Similarly, hours of museum openings on Shabbat are not listed. Only restaurants and snack bars with *kashrut* supervision by a recognized rabbinic authority are included; these listings are kept to a minimum.

Several sites near Jerusalem but not within the city boundaries will be included in a future volume.

Acknowledgements

The author wishes to thank the Jewish Tribune, published in London, for permission to use adaptations of articles originally written for "Annals of a Traveler," a column that appears in the newspaper.

Table of Contents

Section I — Background Information

Facts about Jerusalem

History

1000 BCE	David conquers Jerusalem
960	Building of First Temple
928	Kingdom divided. Jerusalem becomes capital of Judea
705	Hezkyiahu starts to fortify city
701	Sancherib threatens Jerusalem
586	First Temple destroyed
538	Return to Jerusalem and building Second Temple. Beginning of Persian Period
445	Nehemiah builds city wall
332	End of Persian Period. Introduction of Hellenism by Alexander the Great
323	Beginning of Egyptian Period
198	Beginning of Seleucid Period
168	Hasmonean Revolt
164	Chanukah. Temple is cleansed
63	Pompey captures Jerusalem
54	Roman Crassus loots the Second Temple
37	Beginning of thirty-three year period of Herod
66 CE	Revolt against Romans
70	Destruction of Second Temple
132	Beginning of three year Bar Kochba Revolt
135	Bar Kochba defeated. Declaration of Aelia Capitolina
324	Christianity becomes the official religion
614	Persians conquer Jerusalem
629	Byzantines return to Jerusalem
638	Omar conquers Jerusalem. Beginning of Umayyad rule
750	Beginning of Abbasid rule
969	Beginning of Fatimid rule
1071	Beginning of Seljuk rule
1099	First Crusade. Temple Mount mosques become churches
1187	Salah-ed-Din conquers Jerusalem. Beginning of Ayyubid rule
1229	Second Crusade. Jerusalem again conquered
1267	Mamluks conquer Jerusalem

15

1517	Ottomans conquer Jerusalem
1538	Work begun to restore Old City wall
1832	Beginning of eight year period of Mehmet Ali of Egypt
1860	Mishkenot Sha'ananim (first Jewish neighborhood outside walls)
1892	Railroad Jerusalem – Jaffa
1917	Surrender of Ottomans. Beginning of British Mandate
1920	Arab riots
1929	Jewish Hebron evacuated after riots
1947	UN Partition decision
1948	Israel Independence
1967	Six Day War. Unification of Jerusalem

Many of the ancient events in this timeline are approximate. Dating is according to secular sources. There are different dates for ancient events according to some rabbinic sources.

Borders

The borders of Jerusalem have changed significantly over the years. During the time of the First Temple the "City of David" was on the slope leading from the Temple Mount down to Silwan. Later the Temple Mount continued to be the focal point of attention, but the residential city moved slightly to the west, then eventually expanded to parts of today's Jewish Quarter and Mount Zion. The much more extensive walls built by King Herod (see "Third Wall") represented politico-military construction and not necessarily actual residence.

The walls of the Old City as they now stand were determined by Suleiman the Magnificent in 1535/6. It was only in the mid-nineteenth century that settlement began outside the walls, both in the Jewish and Arab sectors.

From 1948 until 1967 Jerusalem was a divided city with the western part ruled by Israel and the eastern section by Jordan. This meant unnatural growth, since population and housing were determined by a ceasefire line rather than by demographic and topographic considerations.

The current municipal boundaries of Jerusalem were more or less set on 28 June 1967 following the Six Day War. Periodic modifications have been made after that date, for example the annexation of parts of Motza in the early 1990s.

The boundaries in the eastern section of the city are contentious in many political discussions, and they in no way reflect Biblical history. Some of the areas included were not considered part of the city under Mandate and Jordanian rule.

Topography

The core of ancient Jerusalem is based on four mountains between which there are three valleys.

- Between the (1) Mount of Olives and (2) Mt. Moriah (Temple Mount) is the Kidron Valley.
- Another valley, that of the "Cheesemakers," lays between the (2) Mount Moriah and the Upper City (in modern terminology the Jewish Quarter) and (3) Mount Zion.
- Between (3) Mount Zion and the (4) New City is the Valley of Hennom.

A good topographic map of the area can be seen in the Tower of David.

Flora and Fauna

There are numerous kinds of flowers and plants that grow in the Jerusalem area. For religious visitors perhaps the several species of plants that grow out of the Western Wall are of particular interest.

1. Henbane (*Hyoscyamus niger*) is the most common plant in the Wall. The plant contains a poisonous, intoxicating substance.
2. Podosnoma (Syrian Golden-drop – *Onosma orientalis*) is a typical rock plant, and is able to penetrate stone with its roots to extract water.
3. Sicilian Snapdragon (*Antirrhinum siculum*) is a wild plant found primarily on the higher sections of the Wall.
4. Horsetail Knotgrass (*Polygonum equisetiforme*) is mentioned in the Talmud as an antidote for snake bites.
5. Thorny Caper (*Capparis spinosa*) produces flower buds used in ancient times as a spice after marinating. Buds open every day in summer months to produce flowers and fruits.
6. Phagnalon (African Fleabane – *Phagnalon rupestre*) is a smaller plant found scattered throughout the Wall.

The birds that are common at the Western Wall are Common Swift (*Apus apus*), known for very short feet, which are used to cling to vertical surfaces. They sleep in the air. These birds are migratory, and return to the same places annually.

Religion

Jerusalem's population has been estimated at approximately 700,000 people, roughly one-third of whom are Arab and two-thirds Jewish. Of the 33 percent non-Jewish population, about 31 percent are Moslem (primarily Sunni), and only 2 percent are Christian.

Buildings

The exterior walls of most buildings are of dolomite limestone, otherwise known as "Jerusalem stone." This was by edict of Ronald Storrs (1881-1955), the second British governor of Jerusalem, who supervised the British master plan for the city drawn up in 1918 by Sir William McLean. Even today city regulations require that all buildings be faced with this stone. There were short periods when there were exceptions, so there are some buildings without the stone. This is most noticeable in the Kiryat Moshe and Talpiyot (original buildings) neighborhoods, which wanted to stress being "suburban."

Street Signs and Names

It has been common practice to use ceramic tiles to display street names in the Old City. The custom started in 1919, when Megherdich Karakashian and several other Armenian ceramic workers came to Jerusalem to renovate tiles in the Dome of the Rock. The Mandate government then commissioned them to make street signs. The custom still continues. Stepan and Berge Karakashian, two brothers, produce the signs at their ceramics store, located at 15 Via Dolorosa.

During the British Mandate many streets in Jerusalem were named after members of the British royal family or after British government personages. After Israel independence, many (but not all) names were changed. Princess Mary Street, for example, became Queen Sholomzion Street. Chancellor Avenue became Rechov Straus.

Today street names are approved by the Jerusalem Names Committee. There is a basic logic. In Geula, for example, many streets are named after the Latter Prophets. The theme of Rechavia is the Golden Age in Spain. Mea Shearim uses the names of Hasidic leaders and rabbis from the old Yishuv (the pre-state Jewish community).

In East Jerusalem there is also a basic logic to street names. In Sheikh Jarrah, for example, many streets are named after famous archeologists.

Archeology

Jerusalem has many archeological excavations. Often excavations cannot be planned. The city's population is growing steadily, and the need to expand the infrastructure of services has meant considerable construction. The Israel Antiquities Authority has had a large number of calls to investigate sites as historic buildings and artifacts have been unexpectedly discovered by construction workers.

Miscellaneous

Visas

Citizens of most English-speaking countries do not need a visa in advance to enter Israel as tourists. Tourists are usually allowed to stay in Israel for six months, which can be extended by applying at the Ministry of Interior in the larger Israeli cities.

Special application is needed for other visas, such as a work permit.

Government Tourist Office

The Ministry of Tourism operates an information office just inside the Jaffa Gate, Sunday–Thursday 0830-1700 (Tel. 02-627 1422). Tourism brochures for sites throughout Israel and maps of the country and selected cities are available in English as well as in other languages.

The Ministry of Tourism also maintains a tourist office at Ben Gurion Airport. They can be reached at telephone *3888 at all hours of the day and night. English is spoken. Information is available on a wide range of topics including hotels and approved taxi fares from the airport.

Security

Entrance into many stores and restaurants as well as into public buildings is subject to security inspection.

There is a rabbinic opinion that certain types of metal detectors (such as those at the entrance to the Western Wall area) may be used on Shabbat. A rabbinic certificate is on display at the approaches to the Western Wall, but a manual search can usually be requested. Details can be obtained by calling Tel. 02-627 3111 before the Sabbath.

All adults are required to carry identification. Allowance is made for those who do not carry even inside the eruv on Shabbat.

Newspapers

The largest circulation local English language daily newspaper is the Jerusalem Post. The International Herald Tribune is sold together with an English edition of Haaretz and can be found at many newsstands.

HaModi'a (Agudat Yisrael) publishes an English-language daily sold in some religious neighborhoods. The main issue of the week is Wednesday.

The [UK] Jewish Tribune can be purchased a day after publication in London at Rosenthal Stationery, Rechov Yishayahu 21, (Tel. 02- 538 4545), just off Kikar Shabbat. The [London] Jewish Chronicle is sold at Steimatzky, Jaffa Road. Tel. 02-625 0155, 02-625 3654.

Time

Israel Standard Time is two hours ahead of UTC. This means that at 12 noon in Israel it is 11 a.m. in Paris, 10 a.m. in London, 5 a.m. in New York, and 2 a.m. in Los Angeles. Time is most often quoted on a twenty-four hour clock (1300 = 1 p.m.).

Israel Summer Time is in effect from the last Friday before April 2 until the last Sunday between Rosh Hashanah and Yom Kippur.

During summer months one should pay special attention to religious calendars (such as candle lighting times) to ascertain if they are on standard or summer time.

Emergency

Twenty-four hour telephone numbers are: Police — 100, Ambulance — 101, Fire — 102. English is not always spoken by the operator handling the call. The Jerusalem Municipality can be reached at 106 from telephones within the city; any number in the city government can be reached through this switchboard.

Disabled Visitors

Equipment for the handicapped (e.g., wheelchairs, crutches, special beds, bathing benches) can be supplied against a deposit by Yad Sarah (02-644 4444), which also operates a fleet of ambulettes for a fee.

Several volunteer organizations provide *gratis* transportation for the handicapped. Shaarei Marpeh (Tel. 02-581 3558) is a Jerusalem charity that operates ambulettes to transport the handicapped for medical treatment and therapy. Ezer MiTziyon (Tel. 02-500 2111) is a larger organization with a Jerusalem branch; in addition to ambulettes, they also provide car service for those needing treatment and unable to go by bus.

To order an ambulette to transport a handicapped person, advance registration is required.

Access Israel (P.O. Box 5171, Kfar Saba 44151) (Tel. 057-7239239) maintains a list of those places in Israel (tourist attractions, wedding halls, etc.) with access for the handicapped. Careful attention should be paid to the date of information, since some reports on Access are not very recent.

Tzevet Telem specializes in tourism for the handicapped. Tel. 02-628 3415/6. They have thirty-five guides trained to provide tourism assistance, either in taking visitors to sites throughout the country or mapping out itineraries.

Business Hours

Commercial businesses are generally open Sunday–Thursday from 0900 until 1900 or 1930. Friday businesses close at about 1400. In the ultra-religious sector businesses tend to open and close slightly later; a break is sometimes taken in the afternoon.

The only bank in the Old City is Bank Mizrachi in the Jewish Quarter. That bank has an ATM machine.

Accommodations

Essentially all Jewish hotels (excluding certain youth-type hostels) have some kind of *kashrut* supervision.

The following are several tourist quality and superior hotels that have mehadrin supervision and a more religious atmosphere on Shabbat:

- Beit Tuvei Ha-Ir, Malchei Yisrael 36. Tel. 02-531 8318.
- Prima Palace (formerly Central), Rechov Pines 2. Tel. 02-531 1811. (Agudah supervision.)
- Reich, Rechov HaG'ay 1, Beit HaKerem. Tel. 02-652 3121.
- Renaissance Jerusalem, Ruppin Bridge and Herzl Boulevard. Tel. 02-659 9999.
- Sheraton Plaza, Rechov King George 47. Tel. 02-629 8666.

Some hotels have electronic or card-code "keys" to open doors. There are also various arrangements for lights and air conditioning to save money and prevent use while the guest is not in the room. Before booking a room for Shabbat at a non-religious hotel, one should verify that there will be no problematic arrangements. Some hotels have Shabbat elevators.

Checkout time for Saturday night should also be verified to avoid extra charges for not vacating at noon as is customary during the week.

Lost and Found

The Police Lost and Found Office is located at Jaffa Road 107, near the Machane Yehudah Market. The office is open Sunday–Thursday, 0900–1600 and before holidays until 1200. It is closed on Fridays and Shabbat.

The building is of historical interest. It was constructed in the nineteenth century and served as the residence of the Noel Temple Moore, the British Consul in Jerusalem (1863–1890). Simcha Janower of Jerusalem sculpted lions at the entrance. The building has been a police station since establishment of the British Mandate.

The Lost and Found office of the Egged Bus Company is located on the third floor of the Central Bus Station. Hours are Sunday–Thursday 0830–1530. Tel. 02-530 4999.

Religious Matters

Sabbath Meals

For those not planning to cook for Shabbat, the standard options are take-out food or hotel dining rooms (advance reservation required for non-guests). Sometimes younger travelers make arrangements with *yeshivas*. "Shabbat restaurants" working on tickets purchased in advanced tend to be a practice of the past.

Sha'atnez

There are some suits and coats that come with a formal certification that there is no *sha'atnez*. These are sold in many stores in the religious areas of the city. In cases where one wants to check independently, or where there is not a proper certificate, the *Eida Chareidit* certifies two laboratories:

- Rechov Mea Shearim 6 (corner Chayee Adam), Tel. 02-537 1021
- Rechov Chana 5, Tel. 1599 500 667

Shabbat Eruv (ערוב)

In very simplistic terms, it is forbidden to carry outside private property on Shabbat. An *Eruv* turns a large area into a "courtyard," thus allowing one to carry within that area on Shabbat.

There are two *eruvin* in Jerusalem. One is administered by the Jerusalem Religious Council; the other (smaller) is under the supervision of the *Eida Chareidit*. Both *eruvin* are checked regularly.

Generally, the Religious Council *Eruv* permits carrying on Shabbat in all Jewish areas of the city with several significant exceptions.

There is no *eruv*:
- Between Neve-Yaacov/Pisgat Zeev and the rest of Jerusalem
- On certain dirt paths behind Ramot
- Between Ramot and Nebi Samwil (Grave of Samuel the Prophet)
- In Lifta
- In the Kidron Valley and on the Mount of Olives

In using the *Eruv*, note:
- The Kiryat HaYovel-Hadassah Ein Karen Road is within the Eruv. Villages off the road are not included.
- In Hadassah-Ein Karem only the hospital/medical buildings and access to them are included. The agricultural school is not included.

For specific questions about the Religious Council *Eruv*, one can call Tel. 02-678 8447 or 052-389 0198.

The *Eida Eruv* covers selected neighborhoods, particularly with ultra-orthodox populations. In some cases the boundaries are the same as with the Rabbinical Council, but in others they are not. Inquiries can be made to Tel. 02-582 5529 or 052-763 6601.

Note: If one decides to use an *Eruv*, this is only to carry items needed on Shabbat. An *Eruv* absolutely cannot be used to bring items needed on a weekday.

T'chum Shabbat (תחום שבת)

On Shabbat it is forbidden for a Jew to venture more that 2000 *amot* (about 960 meters or 0.59 miles) outside the city. That limit is called *T'chum Shabbat* (Sabbath Boundary). Determining that boundary is a very complex halachic task, and the Jerusalem Rabbinate has chosen not to publish any detailed map. To determine if a specific point is within Shabbat boundary, one can call Tel. 02-678 8447 or 052-389 0198.

Nebi Samwil, just beyond Ramot, is an area where this question is frequently asked. Although Nebi Samwil is outside the *Eruv* for the purpose of carrying, it is within Shabbat Boundary.

Yom Tov Sheini (יום טוב שני)

People whose primary residence is abroad and are in Israel only on a visit (even long-term) are generally obligated to keep the second days of holidays as is the custom outside Israel. In case of doubt, a rabbi should be consulted.

Minyanim

Finding a minyan for the second day of a holiday is sometimes a matter of luck. Places to look are hotels with foreign tourist clientele, the Great Synagogue, and the Western Wall. Many of the religious neighborhoods have these minyanim on an informal basis depending on who happens to be there for the specific holiday.

Simchat Torah – Hakafot

A relatively new custom in Jerusalem is for Israelis to hold *"Hakafot Shniot"* (Second *Hakafot*) on the evening after Israeli *Simchat Torah*. This, of course, coincides with Simchat Torah abroad. Since this is not a holiday in Israel, the *Hakafot* are usually accompanied by music. Times and locations can be found in the newspapers.

In recent years some rabbis have banned public *"Hakafot Shniot"* because of inappropriate behavior.

Purim

The exception to the above rule is Purim, when one keeps fourteenth or fifteenth Adar (II) depending on where he is located at sunrise on those days and not based upon where he lives.

As a rule, if someone, even a permanent resident abroad, intends to be in Jerusalem on both days, he keeps only the fifteenth. If he is in Tel Aviv for the fourteenth and Jerusalem for the fifteenth, he keeps both days.

For other ancient cities or for resolution of complicated travel scenarios, a rabbi should be consulted. If a person is in doubt whether he should keep one or two days of a holiday, competent religious authorities should be asked.

Meimuna

The *Meimuna* is a Moroccan and general North African custom that has become very popular in Jerusalem. After the last (seventh) day of Passover, families eat meals highlighted by traditional foods and fancy pastries. The largest public *Meimuna* celebration is usually in Sachar Park.

Asking a Rabbi

The Jerusalem Rabbinical Council can answer questions on mornings and afternoons on Tel. 02-621 4848. The person answering will direct the question to the appropriate rabbi. *Kashrut* inquiries can be made directly to Tel. 02-621 4828.

The *Eida Chareidit* has telephone numbers for asking questions. *Kashrut*: Tel. 02-670 0200. Other matters during afternoons through very late evenings: 02-625 2808; the phone number of the rabbi on duty will be supplied.

Bet Yosef, following the halachic rulings of Rabbi Ovadia Yosef, is located at Rechov Canfei Nesharim 7 in Givat Shaul. The phone number is 02-652 0220.

An interesting telephone service for asking questions is provided by *Kav Yashir*. Each hour from 0700 until 0200 a rabbi is available to answer questions. Just call 05-731-731-XX (XX are the two digits at the beginning of the hour); for example, at 3 p.m. (1500) call 05-731-731-15.

Kashrut questions about products under the supervision of Rabbi Shlomo Machfud can be answered by calling 03-676 5888.

The telephone number for Belz, located at Rechov Dover Shalom 126, is 02-501 6777.

Although Rabbi Avraham Rubin is in Rechovot, many products and restaurants under his supervision are to be found in Jerusalem. The telephone number is 08-939 0816.

Other commonly needed telephone numbers for halachic questions are:

- Rabbi Landau   03-579 1595
- Chasam Sofer – Bnei Braq   03-618 3572
- Chasam Sofer – Petach Tikva   03-931 7040
- She'erit Yisrael   03-677 3330
- Agudat Yisrael   02-538 5252

Some people prefer to confer with a specific rabbi, particularly a highly esteemed figure, concerning their personal questions. If you do not know the rabbi personally, one can use the services of someone to make an appointment. This should be done only when dealing with extremely serious and difficult matters.

Candle Lighting Times

In Jerusalem Ashkenazim light candles before Shabbat and Holidays approximately forty minutes before sunset. These times are published in Friday newspapers. There are Sephardim who light candles twenty minutes before sunset. If a candle lighting time for Jerusalem is given without further qualification, forty minutes can be assumed.

Calculating Sunrise

Sunrise can be calculated according to the astronomical rise of the sun or according to the moment when the sun is seen at the horizon. There can be a difference of several minutes.

The two most common methods of calculating sunrise for Jerusalem are those of Yechiel Mikhal Tucazinsky (1872–1955) and

Moshe Shapira[1], who designed the sundial on Zohorei Hama (see entry).

Parshat HaShavua Reading

When the second day of Pesach or of Shavuot falls on Shabbat, the regular Torah portion is read in Israel, since that day is not a holiday. This causes a difference from communities abroad, where a holiday portion is read. Certain hotels sometimes have *minyanim* with the reading for abroad.

Weekly Pages

Today there are dozens of Parshat HaShavua pages published throughout Israel. Some have national distribution, while others are given out only locally. Virtually all are distributed *gratis*, but there often is a charge for mailed copies (e-mail is usually *gratis*). The pages are to be found in many synagogues, most often on Fridays.

Although the vast majority of pages are in Hebrew, there are several in English and other foreign languages. The most common pages in English are: Torah Tidbits (02-566 7787), Machon Meir (02-651 1906), Midei Shabbat BeShabbato (02-651 9502), and KinderTorah (02-585 2216).

Meorot HaDaf HaYomi (03-577 5333) deals with the week's Talmud pages; both Hebrew and English editions are available.

Some sheets are available on Internet.

Genizah

There are numerous bins in various neighborhoods. The service is run by private organizations and involves a fee (schedule posted on the boxes).

Classes and Lectures

There are numerous classes and lectures open to the general public and appropriate for religious people. A source for sessions in English is Torah Tidbits, the weekly publication of the O-U Center.

Funerals

Funeral parlors most commonly used are at Shamgar (next to Shefa Mall) and Har HaMenuchot. In Israel there is very limited seating at the funeral par-

---

[1] Not to be confused with Moses Wilhelm Shapira who lived in what became the Ticho House.

lor. Most people stand. The major exception is the funeral parlor on the grounds of *Eretz Chaim* (Tel. 02-991 1446), the American cemetery in Beit Shemesh.

Cemeteries

Civilian cemeteries currently in common use are the Mount of Olives and *Har HaMenuchot*. The Mount of Olives is impractical to reach by public transportation, although some parts are serviced by Bus No. 43..

There is some bus service (No. 29 from the Central Bus Station) to the entrance of *Har Hamenuchot*, there is no internal bus service in what is a very large cemetery.

Mount Herzl is used to bury people in the security services (military, police, and fire) and public personages. Numerous busses stop outside; most frequent are Nos. 18, 20.

Eretz Chaim has reasonable bus service to the entrance on the main road, but from there it is a long trek uphill to the cemetery.

Mikvah

Men

Most religious neighborhoods have a *mikvah* open in the mornings and *Erev Shabbat* in the afternoon for men only. One can call the Jerusalem Religious Council, 02-621 4890, to locate such a *mikvah*. Payment usually ranges from NIS 5 to NIS 15 for one-time use (less expensive with a monthly pass). Many places use a coin-activated turnstile that accepts one coin exact payment. In most cases neither towel nor soap is provided. Use on Shabbat is most often *gratis*.

Women

The Jerusalem Religious Council maintains more than thirty *mikvas* for women throughout the city. These are all open to the public; a fee for use is charged and should be verified in advance. To find the closest mikvah, call Tel. 02-621 4890. In addition there are numerous *mikvas* operated by private organizations.

There are two *mikvas* designed for handicapped women. A crane-like apparatus is available at Rechov Elisha 10, Musrara. Tel. 02-627 2008. A *mikvah* for less severely handicapped women is located at Rechov Mazal Tale 1, Pisgat Ze'ev. Tel. 02-656 1951. The Baka *mikvah* for handicapped women is closed.

Kashering Utensils

On the Friday before Rosh Chodesh (a full week before if Rosh Chodesh is on Shabbat) the Eida has a series of locations for the kashering of utensils. A fee is charged.

Belz has kashering every Friday in two locations. The Belz headquarters should be contacted, since hours change according to season.

There are utensils sold with a *hechsher* that kashering is not required before use.

Synagogues

Minyan "factories"

There are numerous places in Jerusalem where one can find a *minyan* at virtually any hour. As one finishes, the next one starts. Some of these "*minyan* factories," as they have become to be known, are:

- Beit Yisrael, Rechov Sonnenfeld 13.
- Belz (scheduled *minyanim* at high frequency), Rechov Dover Shalom 2, Kiryat Belz.
- Geula (Mincha, Maariv), Rechov Malchei Yisrael 6. Afternoon–Evening.
- Mussayif, Rechov Yoel 25, Bukharian Quarter (Tel. 02-582 7276). Sephardic rite.
- Or Tsafon, Rechov Aminadav near Rechov Bar Ilan.
- Zichron Moshe (officially Ohalei Yaacov), Rechov Zichron Moshe.
- Zohorei Chama Sephardic rite, Jaffa Road opposite Machne Yehudah. There is also, of course, the Kotel.

Cohanim

General

General questions about problems encountered by Cohanim can be answered by calling the Cohanim Purity Union at Tel. 02-586 2153 during evening hours.

Birkat Cohanim

In Jerusalem there is *Birkat Cohanim* every morning, at Mincha (קטנה) on fast days, and at *Ne'ila* (not *Mincha*) on Yom Kippur.

There is a custom at the Western Wall to have a large-scale *Birkat Cohanim* in *Musaf* on the first day of what is *Chol HaMoed* abroad and that does not fall on Shabbat. Usually, several hundred *Cohanim* recite the blessing in unison.

Museums

Most Israeli museums make a concerted effort not to have human remains that would prevent a *Cohen* from entering. When there is any doubt, the museum should be called in advance.

Graves outside Cemeteries

There is a difference of opinion whether the bodies of non-Jews can create *tum'at ha'ohel* (impurity) for a *Cohen*. For those who adhere to the stricter ruling, a more stringent consideration of archeological museum visits should be considered. It is also probably better to avoid certain streets because of trees that sometimes overhang. A permanent problem is entering certain Moslem houses in the Old City, particularly in the Moslem Quarter. During the Mamluk era it was common to bury a revered sheikh inside a *madrasah* (school or house of religious study). Most of these buildings have been converted into residences, with the burial room closed.

Cemeteries

The Mount of Olives and *Har HaMenuchot* are divided into sections that are run by the various burial societies. Each theoretically has designated paths permitted for *Cohanim*. Before venturing on the cemetery to visit a grave, a *Cohen* should check with the appropriate burial society.

Kashrut

Mehadrin (מהדרין) and "Regular" Rabbanut (רבנות)

There are significant differences between regular and *mehadrin* kashrut supervision. The tourist should consult with his rabbi to determine which is more appropriate for him. It should be stressed that both are kosher and answer the requirements of Jewish Law. *Mehadrin* is more strict.

In Jerusalem regular supervision means that the Rabbinate is obligated to accept all products carrying the approval of the Chief Rabbinate except meat items and vegetables that have the possibility of bugs or worms. In *mehadrin* supervision this caveat does not exist, and the Rabbinate can reject products that do not meet its standards.

In regular supervision the Jerusalem Rabbinate usually relies on unannounced visits of the supervisor. In mehadrin supervision it is more common to have a permanent supervisor on premises (depending on the product and circumstances).

The liquid milk in all Israeli products under rabbinic supervision is *cholov yisrael* (under supervision from the time of milking). In regular *Rabbanut* supervision powdered milk is not necessarily *cholov yisrael* unless specifically labeled; powdered milk is *cholov yisrael* in *mehadrin* products. In the case of milk *mehadrin* also means that there was no violation of Shabbat in taking the milk from cows.

It should be noted that there is no standard definition of *mehadrin*. The various supervisions use the word as they decide. As is a general rule in Kashrut, one must be familiar with the standards of the organization giving supervision.

Pas / Bishul Yisrael (פת – בשול ישראל)

All products made under official rabbinic supervision in Israel are *Pas Yisrael* or *Bishul Yisrael*, whichever applies. Mehadrin products are usually more stringent in defining when *Bishul Yisrael* is necessary.

Wine

In addition to familiar Israeli wines, recently numerous smaller wineries have opened. Some are totally independent; others use a larger winery

33

for distribution. The products vary in type and quality, and there are even wines produced from organically grown grapes.

Unfortunately, there is no basic rule to identify *mevushal* (cooked) and *non-mevushal* wine. With each brand the *mashgiach* of the winery must be queried.

Warning: There are imported wines that are sold with no rabbinic supervision. There are also two non-Jewish companies, one in Beit Jala and the other a monastery in Latrun, which make wine and sell it in some Israeli stores. These wines are absolutely non-kosher.

On the Airplane

When departing Israel one can order meals with *Eida* supervision from almost all of the regular airlines. Some of the charter companies will take the order, but they claim when queried that providing the meals is not their responsibility.

Note that on El Al all regular meals are prepared under rabbinic supervision, but there is no supervision for the on-board microwave ovens where they are heated. Kashrus and other religious questions on El Al can be directed to their rabbi, Yohanan Hayut, Tel. 03-971 7428 or 050-645 8560 (mobile).

On incoming flights airlines use food supplied at the point of departure. Ordering even a *mehadrin* meal of some carriers does not mean that the meal is necessarily acceptable.

Pesach Books

Several of the Kashrut organizations (e.g., Belz, *She'erit*, and *Eida*) publish annual guides (in Hebrew) that are sold in stores before Passover. Some books come out literally two or three days before the holiday. These volumes cover activities during the year with emphasis on Pesach. In addition to listing approved products, other topics are covered such as eruv maps, koshering utensils, *mikvahs*, and year-round kashrut.

The Jerusalem Rabbinate publishes a *gratis* guide in limited quantity; it can be obtained in their offices at Rechov HaHavatzelet 12, Jerusalem, during office hours.

Passover

Passover products usually are sold from about Rosh Chodesh Nissan. For those people who cannot eat wheat matzos for medical reasons, spelt matzos without gluten (supervision of Rabbi Yehudah Gruber of Williamsburg, Brooklyn) are available by calling 02-500 1854.

Sh'murah matzos from Matzos Yerushalayim are whole wheat.

After Passover

The Rabbinate issues certificates to businesses attesting that they have sold their *chametz* before the onset of Passover.

There is a common custom in certain circles not to eat *chametz* that was produced before Passover, even though it was sold to a non-Jew for the holiday. For this reason there are products that are labeled, "Made from wheat ground after Passover." Particularly on cereals the date of production can be determined by contacting the manufacturer and finding out when the product was manufactured based upon date of expiry.

A variation on this custom is products (mostly pasta and cereals) labeled, "Made abroad and bought by Jews after Passover."

Laws Pertaining to the Land of Israel

Shemitah (שמיטה)

Most food grown in Israel during *Shemitah* is governed by *Heter Mechira* (selling the land to a non-Jew for the *Shemitah* year). Products with "regular" *Rabbanut* supervision can be assumed to be *Heter Mechira* if the products were grown during the *Shemitah* year.

There are some green grocers who sell products which are *Otzar Beit Din*. Special rabbinic laws apply.

Most *mehadrin* food uses produce that is grown in Israel on land that is permanently owned by non-Jews, that is grown in areas not governed by the laws of *Shemitah*, or that is imported from abroad.

It is the opinion of the Chazon Ish that *Shemitah* restrictions apply to all produce grown within the boundaries governed by *Shemitah*, even on the land of a Gentile.

If you are in Israel during *Shemitah* (or the following year), it is suggested that you seek rabbinic advice as to what to do.

Chadash (חדש)

Mehadrin products are certified not to be *Chadash*, grown either in Israel or abroad. "Regular" rabbinic supervision allows *Chadash* grown abroad.

Tithing

Today tithing (*t'rumah* and *ma'aser*) is a rabbinic obligation and not a Torah commandment (according to most opinions). It applies to virtually all produce grown in Israel that is not eaten in the fields.

There are two systems of tithing. In *mehadrin* products the tithing is done from produce physically present. In some localities "regular" supervision allows tithing of produce not necessarily present at the time that tithing is done.

B'chorot

The recognized *mehadrin* supervisions all certify that slaughtered animals do not fall into the category of *B'chorot*, which is forbidden. In the Jerusalem Religious Council problematic animals are sold to a non-Jew in ceremonies held twice a year; in this way the problem is avoided.

Orlah

Fruits grown from trees in the three years after planting are forbidden to eat. Another restriction precludes eating fruit from the fourth year. With some fruits the trees simply do not produce edible fruits in their first years. There are, however, some trees that are problematic. *Mehadrin* stores do not sell fruits which might well be *Orlah*.

Events

Weddings

If you are invited to a wedding during your stay in Jerusalem, the customs are often rather different than those encountered abroad.

Perhaps most striking, there is not always a request for RSVP, although responses are becoming more frequent. Sometimes, personal invitations are not handed out; it is considered sufficient to post a single invitation for "the neighborhood" on a synagogue bulletin board.

The hour for which a wedding is scheduled is not necessarily the hour that the wedding ceremony will be held. It is always best to verify if the actual ceremony will start before sunset or after nightfall.

During the ceremony it is customary for most people to stand. Chairs are usually provided only for the ill and elderly.

By rabbinic decision all weddings must be kosher, and the *chuppah* must meet Orthodox standards. Despite these rules the rabbinate has not been able to stop other practices such as mixed dancing.

There are halls which allow outside caterers. In such instances the specific wedding should be cited when calling to ask questions about kashrut supervision.

Music

In many Jerusalem halls music must stop at 11 p.m. by city ordnance. Even when this does not apply, weddings are most often over by that hour.

There is a customs in Jerusalem not to have music because of mourning for the Temple. Virtually all people say this applies only to the Old City, but there is a small minority which contends that the custom applies to the entire city (in which case only drums are used).

Getting Around

Walking and Hiking

The Israel Path, the main hiking route from the Lebanese border to the Egyptian border, passes through the Judean Hills to the west of Mevasseret Zion, but it never reaches Jerusalem. A new Jerusalem Path has been marked, starting at Ammunition Hill and ending at the Menachem Begin Heritage Center.

Popular with tourists is a five kilometer hike and bike path in Gan Sachar going from the Berlin Center near Beit Hachayal (Soldier's Home) to Patt Junction, with "detours" to sites such as the Supreme Court and the Israel Museum. Problems with the path are unclear directions in certain segments and a lack of distance markers. There is bus transportation back to town from Patt Junction for those who would prefer an easier return.

There are several neighborhood walking paths marked out in the city. Most popular are the Ramot, Gilo, and Pisgat Ze'ev areas. Although these paths are primarily designed for exercise, they provide a good introduction to the neighborhoods. The Gilo path, in particular, which follows the higher elevations and provides scenic panorama views toward both Jerusalem and the outskirts of Bethlehem. The paths vary in length and take from approximately thirty to ninety minutes walking at a brisk pace.

Every year during Chol HaMoed Succot thousands of walkers come to Jerusalem along paths (one longer, one shorter) selected each year and ending in Gan Sachar. The event is known as the "Tsa'adah," in which Jews and non-Jews participate. Some people march in groups. Others walk the route alone or with friends. Souvenir certificates of participation are available, when arranged in advance. In recent years a large number of non-Jewish groups has participated in the march and parade following. This has led many rabbis to discourage (if not totally forbid) Jewish participation.

Local Busses

General

All local bus service in Jewish Jerusalem and most out-of-city lines are run by the Egged co-operative. Lines to Bnei Braq are shared with Dan (tickets are interchangeable between the two companies); other companies

41

service parts of Beit Shemesh, Modi'in/Kiryat Sefer and Beitar/Beitar Illit; these companies do not provide service on Shabbat. Egged and Dan do run tourist busses on Shabbat.

Many inter-city bus lines use the Central Bus Station on Jaffa Road as their hub. There is another hub used by many *mehadrin* busses at Hat Hotzvim on the Ramot Road (Shderot Golda Meir).

Friday Afternoon

Busses in Jerusalem stop gradually before Shabbat and resume Saturday evening. The same is true for *Yom Tov*. When planning a bus trip close to Shabbat, it is best to check when the last bus runs.

Rabbis ask that travelers to Bnei Braq leave Jerusalem no later than two hours before onset of Shabbat.

Saturday Night

The first busses on the Egged No. 1, No. 2, and No. 3 lines from the Western Wall are with payment on Sunday (on the honor system); if you use this service, on Sunday pay any Egged driver or have a multi-ride ticket punched an extra time. Note that because the busses do not leave their garages until Shabbat is over, it takes some time (usually about forty-five minutes) for them to arrive at the station near the Western Wall.

Mehadrin Busses

In these busses men are expected to sit in the front and women towards the back. This separation applies to married couples as well. The word *"Mehadrin"* is usually placed on the front window of these busses. Common *mehadrin* busses are 1A, 3, 15A, 40, 49A, 56, 402 (Bnei Braq), 417 and 418 (Beit Shemesh), 982 (Tsfat and Meron).

Light Rail

A light rail service is being constructed for Jerusalem. At the time of this writing its scheduled opening is on 8 September 2010, but the date is uncertain, since it has been delayed several times. When it does open, the bus lines for Jerusalem will be revamped.

One symbol of the light rail system is the String Bridge designed by Santiago Calatrava (1951-   ) of Spain. The bridge, designed to recall David's Harp, will enable the turn between Rechov Yafo and Shderot Herzl.

Vans

Eisenbach (Tel. 02-537 1144) provides regular van service (*sherut*) to Bnei Braq from Rechov Straus. Prices are either by vehicle or by seat. Unaccompanied parcels are also accepted, with the option of delivery to a specific Bnei Braq address or pick-up at the station (less expensive).

Touring

Fees

Most museums in Jerusalem have fees, which are sometimes substantial. For those travelers on a limited budget discretion is recommended before trying to see every site. On certain occasions (e.g., intermediate days of Succot and Pesach, Independence Day) there are reduced prices or *gratis* admission.

A recent program to reduce fees is the introduction of HolyPass Sm@rt Chip, which enables entrance to five sites in the Old City, discounts in shops and restaurants, and priority for Western Wall Tunnel tours. The cards sell for Adults NIS 99, Children NIS 50.

Section II — Touring Jerusalem

Old City

Overview

Today's Old City is divided into four Quarters: Armenian, Christian, Jewish, and Moslem. These names are more historical than currently descriptive.

All residents of the Armenian Quarter are Armenians, since the area is essentially a monastery, which owns and controls even the stores and the parking lot. There is a museum (currently closed for rennovation) and a library in addition to a church and residences.

The Jewish Quarter has a handful of non-Jewish residents and one bakery owned and operated by non-Jews.

The majority of residents in both the Christian and Moslem Quarters are Moslem, though there are some Jewish buildings in each. The Christian Quarter does have a large Christian presence, because of the Church of the Sepulcher.

Western Wall Area

Temple Mount

The first mention of the Temple Mount in the Torah is Mount Moriah, where Abraham brought Isaac to be sacrificed. The mountain is later mentioned numerous times in connection with the conquest of Jerusalem, the building of the First Temple by Solomon, and in later years the Second Temple.

The Temple Mount is encircled by the Western Wall (commonly called the "Kotel"), the Southern Wall, and the Eastern Wall. The original Northern Wall was destroyed probably during the early Middle Ages, when area was added to the north. An indication of this addition is that Temple Mount was a square, 500 x 500 cubits (*Mishnah Midot* 2:1); the currently enclosed area is a much longer rectangle due to that northern addition. The addition has no holiness for Jews.

The two most prominent structures on the Temple Mount today are the Al-Aqsa Mosque with its silver dome and the Dome of the Rock covered by a gold dome. Al-Aqsa is the third holiest place in Islam, thus the intense Moslem interest in what they call "Al-Haram Al-Sharif" ("Noble Enclosure"). Archeological findings after fires in Al-Aqsa during the Mandate period suggest that the mosque is built on the ruins of a Byzantine church.

Viewing the Temple Mount

Today virtually all rabbis forbid entry into the Temple Mount, since we are all ritually impure. The prominent Rabbi Yosef Sholom Eliashiv (1910–), for example, is stead-fast in his *Halachic* opposition to Jews entering the Temple Mount. The very few religious Jews who do enter, often restricted by political authorities, feel that they are walking only in that area permitted to those who are ritually impure.

There are several vantage points from which the Temple Mount can be seen without halachic problem.

An impressive overview from the south can be enjoyed from the Promenade in Armon HaNatziv (see the section below).

A much closer place from which the Temple Mount can be seen is to the west on the Mount of Olives (no regular Egged bus service). *(See color*

51

plate 2, p. 98) It is on the Mount of Olives that the red heifer was brought (*Mishnah Parah* 3:7). A condition of the sacrifice was that it be in view of the Temple Mount. The Eastern Wall of the Temple Mount is, therefore, much shorter than the Western. Reminder: Jewish Law forbids *Cohanim* to be on the Mount of Olives, since it is a cemetery. For *Cohanim* a similar but slightly more distant view can be had from Mount Scopus.

An alternative to the outdoor vantage points is the Hecht Synagogue at the Hebrew University on Mount Scopus. There is a very impressive view of the Old City with a good glimpse at the Temple Mount through a large picture window.

Beit HaTzalam at Rechov Sheikh Rikhan 42 provides a view of the Temple Mount from the north. The building was purchased by Jews in the 1990s as part of a program to enlarge Jewish presence in the Moslem Quarter.

The place from which one can see the Temple Mount from the East is on the roof of the Breslov Yeshiva located on Rechov Ma'aleh Chaldieh. The yeshiva, occupying the building since the 1980s, welcomes religious visitors. It is, however, awkward and often impossible for women to visit during hours of learning, since the path to the roof is through the *Beit Midrash*.

Another possibility is the roof of a Jewish residential building across the street and two or three meters (ten feet) away. Its drawback is that children often use a playground on the roof (well-fenced), making concentration on any prayer quite difficult. Entry to the building requires approval of the security guard.

Gates to the Temple Mount

There are numerous gates leading to the Temple Mount. To the north the Gate of the Tribes, the Gate of Forgiveness, and the Dark Gate are open. On the west are the Gawanimma, Majles, Iron, Cotton Merchants Gate, Purification, Chain (Shalshelet), and the Moghrabi Gates. For many years non-Moslems were permitted to enter the Temple Mount only through the Moghrabi Gate, which is now being rebuilt after the ramp leading to it started to crumble. Chain Gate (perhaps the Kiponos Gate of the Second Temple period) has also been used as the entrance for non-Moslems.

Today all of the other gates to the Temple Mount are closed. The Gate of Mercy (Rachamim) on the eastern wall, for example, is sealed. On the southern wall the Hulda Gate and its parts are sealed. There are partial remnants of three other Second Temple Period entrances on the Western Wall—Warren's Gate, Barclay's Gate, and the Gate above Robinson's Arch.

Under the Temple Mount

What lies under the Temple Mount is a question that has intrigued Jews and archeologists for centuries. Today there are some very partial answers.

As a paratrooper in the IDF during the Six Day War, Rabbi Yisrael Ariel entered the area under the Temple Mount in the section known as Solomon's Stables. The underground "Stables" received the name from Christian Crusaders. Ariel describes archways, a decorative ceiling, a large hall, and a wide passage way leading to the Hulda Gates on the southern retaining wall of the Temple Mount. Ariel feels that this area is a remnant dating back to the period of the Second Temple. There is, however, no archeological reason to associate this area with the underground space mentioned in the Mishnah (*Parah* 3:3; also see *Mishnah Torah*, *Beit HaB'chirah* 5:1).

There are large stones with loops typical of those used to tie horses. Another opinion, based upon the size of the stones used and architectural characteristics, is that the area was built during the eighth century by the Islamic ruler, Abdul Malik (646–705).

The entrance to the Stables is first mentioned in eleventh century travel literature. The five-by-six meter entrance was restored in Ottoman times, but the large hall apparently went without use. If anything, the hall became home to numerous pigeons. In 1992 the Supreme Moslem Council rejected suggestions to transform the hall into a museum or library.

In 1967 Israeli soldiers did not find any remnants from the Second Temple, nor have others reported findings to the Antiquities Authority. From time to time shallow digging has been performed on the Temple Mount in conjunction with utility lines. Nothing has been uncovered. The Romans destroyed Jewish Jerusalem with a vengeance. Large stones were hurled down from the Temple Mount. The destruction of the Temple was total. Nothing remained.

Western Wall Tunnel *(See color plate 3, p. 98)*

The Western Wall Tunnel dates to the Mamluk conquest of Jerusalem in 1267 and an ambitious building program in the first half of the fifteenth century. The Mamluks had been a subjugated people who embraced Islam, overthrew their masters, and ruled the area from Egypt through Syria with religious strictness and intolerance. They were ousted from Jerusalem in 1488 by the Mongols, who were in turn defeated by the Ottomans in 1517.

Until Mamluk rule a deep valley separated the Temple Mount from the Upper City (today's Jewish Quarter). The Mamluks wanted level streets, so that residents would not have to ascend steep inclines to reach the mosques that had been constructed on the Temple Mount. So, they built a vast network of arches, one atop the other, until a flat passage was achieved.

The idea of forging a connection to the Temple Mount was not new. A more modest single arch had been constructed in the period before the Destruction for exactly that purpose. The remains, attached to the Western Wall, are popularly known as Wilson's Arch, named after an Englishman, Charles William Wilson (1836–1905), who discovered and explained the remnants of the structure in 1864.

Excavation of the Mamluk arches down to the original Roman street has produced what is known as the Western Wall Tunnel, at a lower level under the current street. That Roman street continued along virtually all of the Western Wall. Some of the street stones can also be seen in the excavations to the south [right] of the Western Wall. Over the centuries the Mamluk arches became cluttered with dirt and other debris, hence excavation was necessary.

On a lower level of the Tunnel below the passage of standard tours, the "Synagogue of Rabbi Yehudah Meir Getz (1924–1995)," the late Rabbi of the Western Wall, is the closest point to the Holy of Holies.

In the Tunnel one can clearly see the variety of stones used to build the 488-meter Western Wall. How were the very large stones moved into place centuries ago without modern power tools? They were probably slid downhill from a quarry near the Antonio (Roman fortress at the northwest corner of today's Temple Mount enclosure) and pushed into place.

One stone, however, is particularly significant. It is not part of the current Western Wall. Toward the northern end of the Tunnel under a transparent floor one can see a stone that had been tossed down and left where it fell, presumably during the Destruction. Under another transparent floor one can also see some of the underground streams that supplied water to the area.

The extreme northern end of the Tunnel moves to the west, away from the wall. There it passes by a series of reservoirs dating to the Hasmonean period. Water stored there was evidentially used for the thousands of pilgrims.

The exit from the Tunnel is on Via Dolorosa, north of the Temple Mount enclosure and its medieval addition. Along that walk at the intersection of Via Dolorosa with Rechov HaGai one can again stroll upon the large stones of the ancient Roman street.

During the Mamluk period the buildings on the new streets were constructed flush against the Western Wall.

Rechov HaShalshelet (Chain Street) became the prime Mamluk thoroughfare leading to Chain Gate and the Temple Mount. One of the buildings on this street is the *Mahkime*, just outside the gate to the Temple Mount. The Mamluks initiated construction in 1427 and finished their work two years later. Over the centuries the building has had several uses, including the seat of the Islamic Court. The front entrance to the *Mahkime* can be seen in the small plaza in front of Chain Gate. (For orientation, that plaza is over the covered segment of the men's section at the Western Wall. It is built above the series of arches that yield the flat street above and the Tunnel below.) A key distinguishing feature that can be seen in the *Mahkime* and other Mamluk buildings is alternating red and white stones around entrance ways.

After 1967 there were incidents of rocks thrown down on people praying at the Western Wall, so the *Mahkime* was taken over by the Israel Police Border Guard.

The price for tours of the Tunnel (Hebrew or English) is NIS 25 for adults, and NIS 15 for children and retired persons. Advance reservations are required. No tours on Shabbat. Tel. 02-627 1333 for group reservations, *5958 for individuals. Tours take between seventy-five and ninety minutes. Provision for the handicapped by prior arrangement. A religious guide can also be arranged. During Chol HaMoed an abbreviated *gratis* tour is sometimes offered without prior reservations; the schedule should be verified.

Chain of Generations *(See color plate 4, p. 98)*

This exhibit began in 2006 as a project by Suli Eliav, taking the visitor on a forty-minute walk through generations of Jewish History, with all exhibits constructed from glass. As the guide explains, the purpose of the tour is not to teach the story of the Jewish people; rather, it is to experience the continuous chain of generations and the centrality of Jerusalem for Jews of all times. Nevertheless, there are archeological artifacts that can be seen through a modern transparent floor—a First Temple era building, a Hasmonean ritual bath, a Roman water tunnel (possibly for drainage) and Mamluk construction. A highlight of the visit is a movie at the end telling the story of a soldier who fought during the Six Day War.

Located near the entrance to the Tunnel Tours. Visits by pre-arranged tours beginning at 0800. Closed Shabbat and holidays. Adults NIS 25, Children/Seniors NIS 15. Handicapped accessible. Tel. 02-627 1333.

Western Wall

Background

The Western Wall extends for 488 meters (1601 feet), of which some sixty meters (197 feet) of accessible space constitute what today is commonly known as the *Kotel*. This includes segments of the wall that have been uncovered and opened to the public in increments since 1967.

The Wall is a reflection of the history of Jerusalem. Older stones are at the base. Large Herodian stones, with their rectangular frame that was the trademark of Herod, are higher. Stones from a later era are atop these. Two excavations in the Men's Section show the depth of the Wall, but depth is a matter of perspective. Today, we stand at the Western Wall on top of centuries of building and landfill. Those excavations really show the height of the Western Wall.

According to most opinions the Western Wall is a retaining wall for the Temple Mount. Most Rabbinic authorities rule that it is beyond the boundaries of the Temple Mount, therefore it is permitted to push a *kvitel* [a note] between the stones.

For centuries Jews came to the *Kotel* to offer their prayers, but that was easier said than done. Anti-Jewish riots, such as in 1921, 1929 and 1936, posed problems. In times of tension and confrontation weaving though the narrow streets of the Old City was dangerous to the brink of impossible; staying at the Wall meant becoming an awaiting target. Nor was Jewish prayer or even presence allowed during Jordanian rule in Jerusalem, despite provisions in the cease fire agreement.

Restrictions implemented by non-Jewish rulers posed problems. During the Mandate, for example, the *Kotel* was controlled by the Supreme Moslem Council. For many years it was forbidden to blow *shofar*. It was also forbidden to place tables and chairs near the Wall. Thus, older people could not remain for long, and Reading of the Torah was particularly difficult. One solution was to have longer prayers and Torah reading in the nearby building today known as the Yeshiva of Rabbi Shlomo Goren (1917–1994), on the roof of which there are now six eternal flames in memory of the Holocaust victims.

Physical space also was an issue. The sprawling *Moghrabi* neighborhood built during the Ayyubid period (1187–1250) reached until just meters before the Wall, leaving only a very small area for prayer. That neighborhood, once filling today's vast plaza in front of the Western Wall, was almost totally razed during the Six Day War on the night of 7-8 June 1967.

Near the wall there are numerous Islamic schools (*medrasat* in Arabic) with places of burial inside; those buried include not only famous historic figures, but also the tombs of Sayyid Hussein bin Ali (1854–1931), (the great-great-grandfather of Jordanian King Abdullah II), and of Abdul Kader Al-Husseini (1907–1948), the Arab champion of the 1948 battle for the Qastel (opposite today's Mevasseret Zion).

Prayers (See color plate 5, p. 99)

Today, the *Kotel* is the symbol of our wailing for the destruction of the Temple—the closest point we can come to what was the center of Jewish worship. It is in this context that many people praying at the Western Wall face not straight forward, but slightly to the left, where the Holy of Holies once stood (in all probability the Dome of the Rock of today).

Prayer at the Western Wall should never be taken lightly. The Wall should never become just another tourist site. As we lament the Destruction we must be thankful that not all was destroyed. Parts of three retaining walls of the Temple Mount still remain as a constant memory of a glorious past. We must also be thankful that only in modern times can we pray at the *Kotel* without restriction, openly as Jews.

Religious Jews staying in Jerusalem and its environs "visit" the *Kotel* more than once during trip. There is an informal timetable that one might consider. *Shachrit k'Vatikin* (at sunrise), *Mincha Gedola* and later *Maariv* tend to attract people who are more serious about praying and not camera-clicking tourists.

Weekdays on which there is *Torah* reading usually draw many less-observant families celebrating *bar mitzvah*; for the most part they arrive mid-morning and station themselves near the *mechitzah* (separation between men and women) and the rear fence.

On certain occasions when there is overcrowding at the Western Wall, prayers are held in the upper plaza. There is a religious opinion held by some that it is best not to pray there, since during usual use the area is for socialization and parties and does not have the holiness of a synagogue.

There are handicapped bathrooms.

Western Wall Plaza

As noted, the Western Wall Plaza was once the *Moghrabi* neighborhood, built during the Ayyubid period. The area takes its name from the Arabic word meaning "western"—no, not west of the Temple Mount, where it is located. Rather, the name is from the homeland of the original

Western Wall Plaza. Archeological excavations where the Police Station once stood

Moslem occupants, Morocco, which is located in the western part of the Islamic world.

The Ayyubids, under the leadership of Saladin (1138–1193), conquered Jerusalem from the Christians of the First Crusade; they were later defeated by the army of the Second Crusade. A remnant of the neighborhood is the Moghrabi Mosque on the Temple Mount, which today houses the Al-Aqsa Museum.

After the Israeli capture of the Old City, Gen. Moshe Dayyan (1915–1981) ordered the destruction of the impoverished houses of the Moghrabi neighborhood quickly under the cover of the night, before there could be international objection. One building was left standing at the end of the area farthest from the Western Wall in the northwest corner of the leveled neighborhood—the "Police Station." The structure had been a private Arab residence under the auspices and ownership of the Abu Meddein "Moroccan" Islamic Council.

The former residents of the Moghrabi neighborhood were declared refugees, and King Hassan II (1929–1999) of Morocco offered to absorb them into his country, their traditional home of previous centuries.

Soon the "Police Station" became an office of the Ministry of Religious Affairs, and then the Israel Police took over most of the edifice and gave it its informal name. In 2007 that building was demolished by construction workers to build a new police station and visitors' center.

As soon as crews started to dig, historic artifacts were found under three or four meters (ten to twelve feet) of landfill.

Unearthed was part of a street similar to the Cardo, beneath which there are the bases of pillars and the floors of several stores. This was evidently a street from the later period of the Second Temple. If one were to continue further south on the street, one would presumably reach the small Roman-era pedestrian gate not far away in the Old City wall.

Numerous Mamluk coins were unearthed, as compared with the very few Roman coins. A possible explanation is that any Roman coins were gathered by the Mamluks. Another reason to be cautious in evaluating the findings is that there is apparently a lower stratum from the First Temple period; it is still being evaluated.

The excavations are continuing and are not yet open to the public.

HaKotel HaKatan

HaKotel HaKatan

Moving northward along the Western Wall, the next significant accessible area of religious interest is a segment about fifteen meters (fifty feet) long just north of Iron Gate. The exposed section of the Western Wall at that point is called "*HaKotel HaKatan.*" Although it is far less popular (and less aesthetic—the pavement is often cluttered) than the large segment of the Western Wall, it is of the same religious significance. It is also closer to the accepted site of the Holy of Holies. Today the area is crowded with structural supports. (Note: To the left of the *Kotel HaKatan* there is a doorway and walkway. These lead to a private residence and should not be entered.)

The buildings to the rear of the passage are further examples of Mamluk construction. The Ribat of Kurt al-Mansuri (opposite the *Kotel HaKatan*) was built in the early Mamluk period as an Islamic hospice for distinguished visitors to Jerusalem. In 1440 a second storey known as al-Jawhariyya was built. Today the complex contains private residences and the Archeology Section of the Supreme Moslem Council (Waqf) on the upper floor.

To Reach HaKotel HaKatan

From the Western Wall turn right (north) through the tunnel exit before the steps. Walk on *Rechov HaGai* until you reach a police station, and then turn right (east). Continue past a building of Ateret Cohanim to the end of the street (prudence says it is better to walk during daylight with a partner) until just before the gate to the Temple Mount, then turn left.

Davidson Center

Although now attention is concentrated on the Western Wall, during the times of both the First and Second Temples the most active area was the Southern Wall between the City of David where much of the Jewish population was concentrated and the Temple Mount. It was through there that most people came to the Temple.

Today the southern segment of the Western Wall and the entire Southern Wall are part of an archeological park administered by the Israel Antiquities Authority and four other government agencies. The Davidson Visitors Centre, a building with multi-media presentations, gives an introduction to the area.

One remnant in the park is a large Second Temple stone that was hurled from the southwestern corner of the Temple Mount, evidently dur-

Davidson Center. Excavations at the southwestern wall of the Kotel ©

ing the Destruction. An inscription in old Hebrew characters suggests that from there a trumpeter announced the approaching of Shabbat.

Only the ritually pure could enter much of the Temple Mount, hence it is not surprising that ritual baths have been found in the area. One ritual bath was very large with both entrance and exit stairs; this is opposite the Western Wall some fifteen meters (fifty feet) before its southern corner, close to a Roman "shopping mall" (row of stores). Another ritual bath, possibly dating back to the First Temple era, can be found on the park perimeter opposite the Southern Wall near its eastern corner.

Buildings protrude southward from the wall. These structures are remnants of an Islamic palace and other non-Jewish buildings. (Tip: Wandering though these remnants is interesting, though perhaps difficult for older persons. To the right signs give visitors a choice of a longer and a shorter route. The shorter route is recommended, except for those with an unusually keen interest in archeology.)

The most notable feature of the Southern Wall is the Hulda Gates (*Midot* 1:3) to the Temple Mount; they have been sealed for centuries. Estimates based on the Mishnah are that the gate to the right was an entrance to the Temple Mount. The two double gates on the left allowed the throngs to leave (see *Midot* 2:2). Exceptions were *menudea* and *avel* (mourner) who entered on the left and exited on the right.

Recently a bulge in the Southern Wall drew much attention. Scaffolding was erected to protect the bulge and prevent collapse. The problem has, in fact, existed for more than one hundred years. Ottoman authorities made repairs in that section of the wall. Is this a new problem? Records are incomplete, and there is no definitive answer. The recent bulge was documented in photographs as early as twenty years ago, and Jordanian engineers worked on a solution in coordination with Israeli authorities—an example of peaceful cooperation.

The Israel Antiquities Authority feels that although the basic problem might have existed for some time, emptying dirt from Solomon's Stables only worsened the situation. The current buildings and walls of the Temple Mount are centuries old; there have been repairs in the past, and there probably will be more in the future.

The Jerusalem Archeological Park is open Sunday–Thursday, 0800–1700; Erev Shabbat and Erev Yom Tov, 0800–1400. Closed Shabbat.

Entrance: adults NIS 30; children and seniors NIS 16. One hour guided tours for NIS 160 must be arranged in advance. A recorded audio tour costs NIS 5. Tel.: 02-627 7550.

A guidebook in English can be purchased for NIS 90 (price subject to change).

Busses: 1, 2, 3, 5, 38, 43.

City of David

Until the 1970s the ancient City of David was a neglected site located outside the city walls and known only from limited early twentieth century excavations and various verses in the Bible. The city is first mentioned in the Torah in Genesis in connection with its king, Malchi-tzedek. Many years later it was conquered by King David, subsequently defended by Hezkiyahu, then eventually destroyed by the Babylonians.

City of David. Ancient tunnel supplying water to Jerusalem (Sheina)

Mysteries hidden over the centuries have begun to be unearthed. Walking through the City of David truly increases religious understanding of the Bible. A three-dimensional movie provides a fifteen minute introduction to the history of the area. The thread line of history is recreated through powerful cinematographic and sound techniques.

Tour

The City of David lies to the south of the Old City wall, dominating an elevated ridge surrounded by valleys, which aided defense. King David evidently built his palace in the northern section of the City of David, near the area where King Solomon would build the First Temple. As you enter the City of David, you walk on a metal grating. Look down at the large thick stones in the archeological excavations below. Archeological techniques verify that in all probability the stones were part of a royal palace.

Area "G" is archeological nomenclature for the area adjacent to the palace. There, Yigal Shiloh (1937-1987) discovered larger than usual buildings with several rooms on the first floor, and stairwells suggesting the existence of a second storey. The working assumption is that these buildings were used by well-to-do people associated with the royal court. In one room, for example, a piece of boxwood furniture was recovered; the probable origin of the wood was northern Syria, giving support to the suggestion of wealth.

One room contained fifty-three seals, including one with the name G'maryahu ben Shafan, a scribe mentioned in Jeremiah 36:10, again reinforcing the theory that the area had a connection to the palace.

Hezkiyahu embarked on a multi-faceted defense plan. Water is always a matter of critical concern. As early as the Canaanite period a long underground tunnel went downhill to a spring, from which fresh water was carried into the city. As warring forces neared the city, Hezkiyahu enclosed the spring inside a fortified area, then he constructed a second and much shorter water aqueduct to the Waters of Shiloach area, so that water could be hauled on outdoor paths within the city. This was a strategic factor in defense of the city.

The Judean king also built the "Broad Wall" as part of the city's fortifications.

Hezkiyahu succeeded in saving Jerusalem from destruction, but in 586 BCE[2], the end of the city came. Babylonian forces laid siege, and defenses crumbled. Destruction was virtually total.

---

[2] Throughout this book the secular date of 586 BCE is used. There is another (rabbinic) tradition of 421 or 422 BCE

In one building in Area "G" archeologists found nine arrowheads (both Jewish and Babylonian). In another room no less than ninety centimeters (thirty-five inches) of ash covered the floor. It was too difficult to clear the stones of the previous city, when Jews returned from Exile seventy years later. There was no choice. Most of the new city was built on a close-by site.

For centuries the ancient water tunnels were dubious legends. In 1909–1911 Captain Montague Parker (1878–1962), a former British soldier, was convinced that the treasures of the Second Temple were buried in those tunnels, and for two years he secretly excavated. But, such efforts could not be kept under wraps forever. When his project became known, it was abruptly halted by Ottoman authorities. As Parker recorded in his diary, he hurriedly left pail and shovel behind.

Following the Six Day War, Israeli archeologists started a systematic scientific effort to unravel the secrets of the City of David. They excavated several areas, and removed dirt from the ancient water system. They did not find the treasures of the Second Temple, but they did find two items—the rusted pail and shovel left behind by Parker!

Today the City of David is not abandoned. Jewish residents fled the wanton violence of the 1929 riots, but in recent years over 250 Jews have moved back. They established a synagogue and a *kollel*. Jewish life has returned.

Directions: From the Western Wall, exit the Old City through Dung Gate. Turn left, then right after twenty or so meters (sixty feet). Entrance to the City Of David is to the left. Hours: Sunday–Thursday 0900–1700, Friday 0900–1300. Closed Shabbat. Entrance: adults NIS 23, children NIS 12, seniors NIS 11.50. Tel. 02-626 2341. Guided tours (highly recommended) are available in Hebrew and English by prior arrangement. Average time of a visit is two hours. Walking, particularly in the water tunnels, can be difficult; comfortable shoes are recommended.

Jewish Quarter

Ariel, Center for Jerusalem during the First Temple

Other nations have been exiled. Other cities have been destroyed. The glory of ancient Rome is a matter of history studied in schools. There are no more Babylonians to recall the magnificence of Babylonia, nor do the Greeks of today have more than a cultural or linguistic identification with the Hellenic Empire of Alexander. Yet, Jews mourn the destruction of Jerusalem. The devastated city is in our prayers and even solemnly remembered during the joy of a wedding. Why? Why is Jerusalem different from every other city? The Ariel Center tries to answer this question by looking at the history and uniqueness of Jerusalem during the First Temple period.

The location of the city, chosen by the Jebusites, was dictated by a water source and the adjoining wadis, the steep decline to which provided protection from foreign armies. By the eighth century BCE the city expanded slightly to the east and significantly to the west (in modern terms the Jewish Quarter and Mount Zion). This is all explained in a large model showing the expansion of the city.

Burial inside the walled city was forbidden for reasons of ritual purity. There are, therefore, more than 120 nearby graves and burial caves, mostly in the Kidron Valley.

The system of burial was different from ours. To maximize space within a cave bodies were left on a slab for a year to decompose. The bones were then collected and buried. In the Center there is a small mockup that illustrates the system. (The best example can be seen in a burial cave on the grounds of St. Étienne on Nablus Road, but a visit is not recommended, since today the area is owned and operated by a Roman Catholic monastery.)

Unlike current practice, it was common to place property in the burial caves. At the Center there is the reproduction of a sign claiming there is nothing than can be robbed from the graves inside the cave. If the thief did not believe the sign and wanted to try anyway, a curse upon him is added—and at that time in history curses were taken very seriously.

Blessings were also taken seriously. The oldest Biblical fragment found, dating back to this period, is *Birkat Cohanim* (the Priestly Blessing), recovered from a First Temple era site.

Idols of worship, similar to those found in the City of David, are on display, a very tangible reminder that idol worship was sadly prevalent during this period. One does not need any more evidence than the constant admonitions of the prophets.

An accompanying film contains a combination of an actor interchanging with animated drawings of Biblical personages. The presentation is shown on two different screens, one standard and one of textured material several meters forward. Between the two screens is the model of Jerusalem. The dialogue presented is with heavy emphasis on Biblical verses.

The bottom line on the audio-visual presentation is an unqualified, "Excellent!" If the entrance fee seems slightly high, it is because of a personal presentation by a guide and recovering the production cost of the audio-visuals.

The Rachel Yanait Ben-Zvi / Ariel Center is located on the corner of Bonei HaHoma and Plugat HaKotel. Open Sunday–Thursday 0900–1600. Closed Shabbat. Advance reservations required. Entrance fee: Adults NIS 18, Children NIS 14. Both the oral presentation and the film are available in Hebrew and English. Tel. 02-628 6288.

Batei Galicia

Walk down Rechov Chabad until you reach a small metal staircase just before the intersection with Chain Road (*Rechov HaShalshelet*). Ascend the steps. You are now on the roof of the market place! If you proceed another ten meters (thirty-five feet), you can look down through security fencing and see Rechov David. Continue until you reach a wooden ramp, then turn right and cross it. In an overlooking security post there is an Israeli guard. This is a small Jewish enclave in the Moslem Quarter—Batei Galicia.

Jewish presence in this area goes back to the mid-nineteenth century, when Jews opened the Tziyon HaM'tzuyenet Synagogue surrounded by some twenty one-room "apartments" occupied by sixteen Jewish families, who came from Galicia. According to records, the residents were tailors and blacksmiths, teachers and students. Sir Moses Chaim Montefiore (1784–1885), in notes from his last trip to Eretz Yisrael in 1875, describes the moral character of the residents. Despite their poverty, they allocated space for receiving visitors. Each traveler was offered *gratis* room and board for three days, with extensions readily available as needed. In 1886 the area, previously rented, was bought and officially became Jewish property.

In 1936 the history of Batei Galicia came to a tragic interruption. During Passover Arabs started what was to be three years of rioting. An order was given to evacuate Batei Galicia for security considerations, and almost all of the families left. Reuven Klepholtz remained. On 13 May 1936

Klepholtz was walking home from the Jewish Quarter. He was shot and stabbed; subsequently, he was buried on the Mount of Olives. Jewish presence in Batei Galicia was no more, and much of the area was destroyed.

In 1982 the Tziyon HaM'tzuyenet Synagogue was restored. Six years later Rabbi Yitzchak Zilberman opened a yeshiva on the site. Families moved into reconstructed apartments. Batei Galicia came back to life. Hebrew letters that designated apartments predating the destruction in 1936 can still be seen over some doorways.

The yeshiva, housed in the Tziyon HaM'tzuyenet Synagogue, has some eighty students, half of them married. They learn in a program that covers an average of a page of the Talmud per day with stress on *chazarah* (review), going over material time and time again. The unique feature is that students wear tefillin during the entire day. Rabbi Zilberman realized that this was an unusual practice, although he felt that it is well-grounded in halachic sources. He sought the advice of Rabbi Shach (1899-2001), *ztz'l*, and he was told that the practice is certainly proper, but it should be restricted to the yeshiva so as not to cause public controversy.

Broad Wall and Israelite Tower

In 1970 Professor Nachman Avigad (1905–1992) of Hebrew University unearthed a portion of the "Broad Wall" as part of the excavations of the Jewish Quarter prior to its reconstruction. Avigad, who had come to Palestine in 1926, dedicated his professional career to archeology. He was quick to realize the importance of his discovery.

This was the first time that the exact northwestern boundary of First Temple Jerusalem could be established. There were various theories about the extent of the city. Now there was finally irrefutable proof. In all Avigad found roughly eighty meters (250 feet) of the ancient wall, which presumably began at the Temple Mount.

In 701 BCE the Assyrian army led by *Sancheriv* invaded Eretz Yisrael, and *Hezkiyahu* decided to build a defensive wall, the "Broad Wall," as part of his plan to protect the city. The king was encouraged by the prophecy of Isaiah that Jeru-

Broad Wall. Two meter thick wall to defend Jerusalem (Sheina)

salem would be saved. Jewish forces held fast against the enemy siege. The Assyrians failed and retreated.

No ruler or military commander likes to admit defeat. In his Annals Sancheriv writes that Hezkiyahu paid a large tax for his army to retreat. Perhaps this was his way of saving face.

Ancient city walls were by no means flimsy. Today's much-discussed Separation Barrier is relatively thin but heavily reinforced. The Broad Wall did not enjoy the benefits of modern technology, so it was built literally stone by stone. Rocks and boulders held together by dirt were amassed to build a wall eight meters (twenty-five feet) tall and almost eight meters thick—certainly impregnable with the weapons of the time. Although the walls of other cities were not as thick, excavations such as Tel Beit Shemesh show that the ancient city walls were impressive. This gives all the better appreciation of the miracle of Jericho's crumbling walls after *Yehoshua's* seven circumambulations.

Later in history, after return from the Babylonian exile, the "Broad Wall" (presumably the same one) was rebuilt as is mentioned in Nehemiah. History of the Second Temple period, though, took a different turn. Jerusalem grew. The population expanded, and new neighborhoods were added. Finally, Herod enlarged the city with the "Third Wall." The "Broad Wall" no longer defended the city.

Two segments of the "Broad Wall" are on view for the public. One is parallel to the Cardo on the upper level; the other portion is several meters away. At the latter site there is a map showing an overlay of the "Broad Wall" on the current Old City and a poll showing the estimated height of the ancient wall.

Visitors should remember the obvious—the boundaries of ancient Jerusalem were very different from the walls of today's Old City.

The Israelite Tower, part of the defenses, is adjacent, and is being renovated.

Rechov Plugat HaKotel corner Rechov Shonei Halachot. No charge. Information can be obtained from the Jewish Quarter Development Company, Tel. 02-628 8141.

Burnt House

As the Jewish Quarter was being reconstructed in 1969, workers reported an archeological find to the Antiquities Authority—the basement floor of an ancient building with a variety of utensils. Archeologists later dated the charred remains probably to the destruction of Jerusalem and the Second Temple era.

The material found was astounding. There was even a stone weight inscribed with the word "Kathros," the name of a family of a priestly family (Pesachim 57a). The artifacts give a keen insight into life at the time of the Destruction.

Today the "Burnt House" (down a long flight of stairs, but wheelchair accessible with a special lift) is open to the public. The museum, however, is disappointing. Artifacts recovered are tastefully displayed in cases with well-designed lighting. Missing, though, are detailed explanations of each item.

Archeologists have decided this was probably the house of the Kathros family. How did *Cohanim* use stone vessels to avoid ritual impurity? (Mentioned in a booklet for sale, but not addressed in the display.) Can anything be learnt about the lifestyle of *Cohanim*? Instead of addressing these questions, the highlight of the museum is a multi-screen historical fiction film (when shown in Hebrew, earphones with English translation are available) describing events in the last days of the Second Temple.

The plot of the film is trite. The older son of Pinchas Kathros switches allegiance from priestly clans willing to accept Roman rule with all of its pleasures for the privileged class, and defects to the Zealots, who have spent several years garnering supplies for the planned Jewish Revolt.

The film drives home, perhaps in disrespectful terms, the utter corruption of the *Cohanim*, and the jealousy and hate rampant at the time. Both of these phenomena are well known from traditional Jewish sources, but it is hard hitting to see them expressed in terms of human interaction. It is particularly disturbing when Pinchas Kathros differentiates between the presumably doomed fate of the common folk and the perceived invulnerability of the *Cohanim*.

A religious Jew would never have written the script of the film. Although many *Cohanim* were corrupt, it is distasteful to attribute concrete deeds to a specific clan, whose name is mentioned in the Talmud, albeit negatively.

The script makes a concerted effort to include references to Biblical verses and religious practice. Yet, there are errors. Kathros' older son, for example, enters the house to find that Romans have slain the family. In a previous scene his father does not want to defile himself by touching his son who is ritually impure, after having killed Romans with his sword. Now the son picks up the cadaver of his fiancée, and leaves the corpses of his parents. At best one can say that this is emotionalism superseding the exactness of religious dictates.

A recommendation to visit the Burnt House is problematic. If a visitor can accept the film as an expression of historical fiction (and not a lesson in

Jewish History or Jewish Law), he will find the issues presented to be intellectually challenging. Otherwise, avoid the museum.

Burnt House is at Rechov Tiferet Yisrael 2. Busses 1,2,3,5,38. Sunday–Thursday 0900–1700 (last film 1615); Friday 0900–1300 (last film 1215). Closed Shabbat. Adults NIS 25; seniors 15; children 12. Tel. 02- 628 7211. Wheelchair accessible by prior arrangement.

Cardo *(See color plate 6, p. 99)*

It is ironic that the Cardo, a central attraction in Jerusalem's Jewish Quarter, is a tragic reminder of the utter destruction of Jerusalem by Roman troops. The devastation wrought by Rome was designed to obliterate Jewish presence, to the extent that a new network of streets was developed, no longer emphasizing the centrality of the Temple Mount. Under Hadrian (76–117 CE) the city's east-west road became the *Decumanus*; the north-south thoroughfare became the Cardo, with a secondary road along what is now called *Rechov HaGai*. The Romans started the rebuilding of the city and its streets, and the Byzantines continued the work.

The Madaba Map, named after a church in Jordan where it was unearthed in 1884 as a floor mosaic, is a key to the understanding of the Cardo. It is the earliest map depicting the city and features the Cardo as the main route from the Nea Church in the south (in the area of today's parking lot in the Jewish Quarter) to the Pillar Gate in the north (today's Damascus Gate, still called by that name in Arabic). For the residents of Jerusalem, the

Cardo. Roman street stones (Sheina)

"center" of town was the Pillar Gate, where public gatherings were held and announcements were made.

The Madaba map is not objective cartography. It is a religious statement of the Church. In the center of the Cardo is the Church of the Sepulcher. Missing?—the entire area of the Temple Mount. The intent was to ignore all Jewish symbols.

The original Madaba Map covers the area from Tyre in the north to Thebes in the south. A replica of a segment of the map, showing just Jerusalem, is on display in the visitor's gallery at the Cardo opposite an audio-visual presentation.

The Madaba map is a statement concerning the middle of the sixth century, when it was made. More or less at that time the Roman Cardo was extended by the Byzantines, from Rechov David (the main street leading to the Jaffa Gate) southwards. It shows that addition.

Rebuilding the Jewish Quarter after 1967 enabled archeologists to excavate part of the Cardo, most of which is still buried under the Arab marketplace. (Segments of Roman street pavement can still be seen on the *Decumanus* in a courtyard near the exit from the Western Wall Tunnels, in the Christian Quarter, and on Rechov HaGai as it intersects with the *Decumanus*.)

Start your visit at the southern end of the renovated Cardo. This was a spectacular road 22.5 meters (73.8 feet) wide, considerably wider than the area open to tourists, lined with five meter-tall (fourteen feet) decorative pillars and stores, embellished by porticos, and continuing 950 meters (3200 feet). There was even a below-ground drainage system for rain water! The archways of two stores can be seen, as well as numerous repaired pillars.

Proceeding northwards is a museum about the fall of the Jewish Quarter in 1948. Slightly beyond and down an awkward staircase are the remains of a Hashmonean era fortress that adjoins what at the time of construction were remnants of the city wall from the period of the First Temple. (Parts of that wall, more than two meters (seven feet) thick, can be seen by going to the parallel Jewish Quarter Street. Turn at the side street with the public bathrooms—wheelchair accessible— then walk for five or six meters (twenty feet).)

Today this section of the Cardo is lined with shops opened in the mid-1980s. During holiday seasons there are often stalls with vendors, trying to recreate the historical era of bustling businesses along the Cardo.

If you proceed through the Arab market, look up to the right. There you can see windows from the plaza outside Batei Galicia (described elsewhere). After a seven or eight minute walk you will reach the Damascus

Gate. Outside to the east there is a museum where parts of the Roman Gate and an impressive plaza (built in the second century CE after the Bar Kochba Revolt) are to be found (see entry).

For inquiries about the Cardo, information can be obtained from the Jewish Quarter Development Company, Tel. 02-628 8141/2. The Roman Gate and Plaza are operated by the Davidson Center.

Herodian Quarter – Archeological Museum

The Roman destruction of Jerusalem was both brutal and devastating. The Lower City was completely destroyed, the Second Temple was demolished, and then on 8 Elul the Upper City was no longer. The remnants on display in the Herodian Quarter Archeological Museum give tangible testimony to opulent life in the Upper City in its days before its capture.

The spacious houses of the Herodian Quarter (including the Burnt House reviewed elsewhere), built during the last two centuries before the Destruction, offered their residents a commanding view of the Temple Mount. It was plush living at its best. Worldly tastes were paramount. Recovered in the archeological excavations are decanters from Rhodes and green serpentine vessels from Egypt. There is also a room decorated in the style of Pompeii.

Lavishness was the theme. To be seen are frescoes on walls, and nine mosaic floors, five of which are in bathrooms. Yet, there was a Jewish aspect to life. The mosaics were all geometric, maintaining the tradition of the time not to reproduce human images.

It is clear that there was no shortage of amenities. A drainage system brought waste to the Kidron Valley. There were also private ritual baths in the houses, so that residents did not have to use the public facilities at the entrance to the Temple Mount. One house apparently had 600 square meters (6450 square feet) on three floors; the basement had storage rooms and baths; the first storey contained a very large reception area and living quarters; and, there was an upper floor.

Herod earned the reputation of having an obsession to build. He doubled the size of Jerusalem, enlarging the city virtually to today's Russian Compound. He built fortresses and palaces in Jerusalem, the Herodian (near Tekoa), Jericho and Masada. But, he was a product of his times. It was an era of building ... at least for the wealthy.

Affluence was not only demonstrated in buildings. Recovered from the Herodian Quarter and in showcases are a sun dial, parts of decorative tables, storage vessels, oil lamps, and serving trays. And, of course, there was money (coins). These all supported a prosperous way of life.

Not all can be preserved in archeological excavations. The Herodian Quarter was built upon previous layers. Parts of First Temple era life were also unearthed. Most interesting is a set of eighth–seventh century BCE jars, imprinted with the word, "*LaMelech*" ("for the king"), and with the names of cities. The jars were used for tax collection. Also found were pottery vessels and oil lamps.

Life in the Upper City was splendid and comfortable, but all came to a tragic end, as Roman soldiers torched the houses of even the wealthiest. The city lay in ruins. In the museum there is a transparent case containing a burnt ceiling beam, a tangible reminder of the destruction of Jerusalem.

Entrance to the museum is through Yeshivat Ha-Kotel on Rechov Ha-Karaim. Open Sunday–Thursday, 0900–1630. Closed Shabbat. Entrance fees: adults NIS 19, seniors NIS 15, children NIS 7. Tel. 02- 628 3448. Guided tours are not generally provided. Thirty minutes should be allocated.

Karaite Synagogue

The Karaites are a sect deviant from normative Judaism. They reject the Oral Law (Talmud). They became strong in the ninth century under the leadership of Anan ben David, who is considered their founder. Their teachings have been rejected by Jews over the centuries, from Saadia Gaon (882–942) to the 1950s failed effort by the Israel Chief Rabbinate to deny them entry into Israel.

Today only one Karaite family lives in the Old City, and its members maintain the Karaite synagogue, once home to a much larger community.

The Karaites contend that Anan ben David built the synagogue on today's Karaim Street, after he came to Jerusalem from Babylonia in the eighth century. It is more plausible, however, that the building was constructed during the Crusader period and was converted into a Karaite synagogue in the late thirteenth century. In any event the building, decorated with a large collection of silver oil lamps and carpets on the floor, is the oldest existent Karaite synagogue. Congregants, usually from Karaite communities outside Jerusalem, remove their shoes before entering, as is the Moslem custom. There is also a Karaite cemetery on Mt. Zion.

A visit to this synagogue is not recommended, given religiously objectionable Karaite philosophy.

Old Yishuv Court Museum

The Old Yishuv Court Museum is laid out chronologically, starting with a room furnished according to the style of the Ottoman period. Don't be fooled. What looks like a sofa is not one. It is a pile of mattresses artfully covered complete with pillows. At night it is taken apart to allow the residents of the one room apartment to sleep, each with a mattress placed on the floor.

Pita bread was a common staple, and it was baked in various shapes (six are on display) primarily according to community. No big matter! The ingredients are the same, and so is the taste.

Life was hard in old Jerusalem. During Ottoman years there was no running water in the city. The rainy season ends with Pesach, and by early summer the wells in the Old City usually dried up. Then water was hauled from Silwan or brought by non-Jews from a water source on the Temple Mount. Although there is a small garden in the courtyard water was too scarce to plant flowers. Spices were grown—for *havdala*, of course!

One room of the museum in particular has a special history. Tradition says it is where Rabbi Yitzchak Luria, the "Ari," was born in 1534. Some two hundred years after his death in 1572, Jerusalem residents established the Ari synagogue in that room. There was no space for a women's section, so on Yom Kippur women prayed outside. In 1936, however, the synagogue ceased to exist. It was torched and totally burned during the Arab uprising. What is on display today is a reconstruction.

The mid-nineteenth century saw the entry of Europeans into Jerusalem, and with them came western culture. Wealthier families brought European furniture into their houses. Even Sephardic families developed European tastes. This trend was only reinforced during the British Mandate.

Mandate years were a time of community growth. One family that came to Jerusalem was Hacohen, immigrants from Pinsk. The husband had been a ritual slaughterer of meat and fowl in Europe, but in Jerusalem he could not find employment. There were no cattle to be slaughtered. The ritual slaughter of sheep was controlled by the Sephardim. HaCohen had a solution to his situation. He received a government permit and started the first Ashkenazi commercial slaughter of chickens in Jerusalem.

The last decade of the Mandate was particularly difficult. After the 1936 Arab uprising mixed neighborhoods became a thing of the past. Arabs left the Jewish Quarter; Jews fled from Moslem areas. Shomrei HaChomot closed its synagogue near Chain Road. Then, after the United Nations vote of 29 November 1947, sporadic fighting intensified. Finally, Jerusalem was under siege. Virtually everyone fought. The secular took up arms next to the religious. On 28 May 1948, however, the Jewish Quarter fell. Arab Legion soldiers demolished building after building.

There are heroes even in the darkest hour. One was Esther Calingold (1925–1948), a volunteer from London who was fatally wounded in the fighting in the Jewish Quarter. She died on 30 May, two days after the cause was lost; her remains were transferred to Israel by the Armenians.

Another hero was Rabbi Yitzchak Danziger. Those Jews who did not evacuate the Jewish Quarter were taken prisoner by the Arab Legion, who asked that prisoners identify themselves. Danziger was the first to step forward. The seventy-five year old rabbi was a proud Jew. He wanted no special privileges.

Life as a prisoner of war was not easy; life as a Jewish prisoner of war was even more difficult. There are several very unique items on display that illustrate the problems of religious prisoners. Rabbi Shlomo Min HaHar, an expert in the Hebrew calendar, was afraid that other prisoners might become confused with dates and not observe holidays. He wrote a two-year calendar, showing which were long and short months, and when religious holidays occurred.

Baruch Chaim Amedi was only seventeen years old, but he had an eidetic memory. He wrote out an entire prayerbook. A page opened to the Additional Service of Rosh Chodesh is on display.

A visit to the museum is definitely recommended. To get the maximum benefit, a guided tour (Hebrew or English) should be arranged in advance (Tel. 02-627 6319). The usual visit takes about one hour.

The museum is at Rechov Or HaChayim 6. Best access is from Jaffa Gate or Bus 38 to the Armenian Quarter stop. Sun–Thurs 1000–1700; Fri 1000–1300; Closed Shabbat and holidays. Entrance fee: adults NIS 14; seniors 7; students 8; families 35. Tel. 02-628 4636. On premises is the Or HaChayim Synagogue (founded 1742), and open without fee.

"One Last Day" Museum

On 28 May 1948 the Jewish Quarter fell to the Arab Legion after a ten- day battle, leaving sixty-nine Jewish dead. (Following the Six Day War, on 4 August 1967, the bodies of many of the dead were retrieved from temporary graves on Rechov Galed and were reburied on the Mount of Olives.)

Those taken prisoner spent the night in the Kishleh, the police station near Jaffa Gate. Most were released and deported through Zion Gate, bur more than 200 able-bodied men were taken to POW camps in Jordan.

One of the misconceptions of history is that those who remained until the last moment were Zionist underground fighters. In all there were only 150 defenders of the Jewish Quarter—and 1600 residents. Amongst those remaining until the very end were the Ashkenazi Rabbi of the Jewish Quarter, Israel Mintzberg, age eighty-three, and his Sephardic counterpart,

Reuven Hazan, age seventy. The vast majority of those who refused early evacuation and stayed were the ultra-Orthodox, including women and children, who surrendered to the Arab Legion on Lag B'Omer. The youngest "fighter" was ten years old. It was the job of children to load ammunition.

There were disappointments. It was to the dismay of the residents that the Palmach broke through Arab Legion lines at Zion Gate and reached the Jewish Quarter, only to withdraw. Why? They were unprepared for their success in breaking through Arab lines!

A tactic used by the fighters in the Jewish Quarter was to run from position to position, in each place firing a round or two, thus fooling the Arab Legion into thinking that the Quarter was being defended by a large force. It was the job of women to make noises from the clinking of metal, another ruse to deceive the attackers about the weapons the Jews possessed.

On the "Last Day" surrender was inevitable. There was virtually no ammunition left. Many of the residents gathered in a Sephardic synagogue, opened the Aron Kodesh (Ark), and recited *Vidui*, then *Shema*. As one person recalled, a little child asked his parents, "What are you doing?" It is hard to forget the answer, "This is what Jews do before we die."

The display in the museum shows photographs taken by John Philips (1914-1996), a reporter/photographer for Life Magazine, as he documented the siege, battle, and fall of the Jewish Quarter. He had full access. He was dressed in a Jordanian uniform and was given permission to wander as freely as battle conditions permitted. Philip's article cites Abdullah Al-Tal (born 1918), commander of the Arab Legion in Jerusalem, and Moshe Russnak, commander of the Jewish Quarter. Russnak was not a professional soldier; in later years he was the owner of a haberdashery shop in the Geula neighborhood. In 1975 Philips was the guest of the City of Jerusalem. He toured the Jewish Quarter, then being rebuilt, and met with some of the people in his photographs. Most moving are the pictures showing intentional destruction. It was the clear aim of the Arab Legion to destroy Jewish life—from houses, to yeshivas, to synagogues.

The museum contains a ten minute movie (Hebrew only) with footage from the fighting of 1948 and recent interviews with some of the Jewish fighters, who recalled the battles. This was Moshe Russnak's last project. He appears numerous times in the film, explaining history and heroism. Several days after the movie was completed, Moshe Russnak passed away.

For those not familiar with the battles of 1948, the museum will be somewhat dry and perhaps unexciting. The film, however, gives insight into the last days of the Jewish Quarter. A longer DVD version is offered on sale, available in Hebrew only.

Open Sunday–Thursday 0900–1700, Friday 0900–1300. Closed Shabbat. Located on the Cardo. Entrance fees: Adults NIS 12, Children NIS 6. Tel. 02-627 3916.

Rechov Plugat HaKotel (Kotel Platoon)

The name of this street has nothing to do with the IDF unit that captured the Kotel in 1967; it goes back to Arab rioting of the 1930s.

A main target of the Arab disorders was the Jewish Quarter. In 1937 anti-Jewish rioting intensified. Beitar placed a platoon of twenty-five "soldiers" in the Jewish Quarter to help defend the area and escort Jews to the *Kotel*. In 1938 rioting continued and the British addressed the problem. Instead of taking action against the rioters, Mandate authorities arrested the Beitar platoon and banned them to enter the Old City. The street is named after them.

Siebenberg House

As the Siebenberg family dug in the basement of their home during a period of some twenty years, they uncovered historical artifacts dating to the First and Second Temple eras. Amongst the findings were remains of residences, a water system, escape tunnels, and even a burial vault. The pottery and other artifacts uncovered confirm what is known from other excavations and sources—the Upper City was home to the wealthy.

The Museum is at 5 Rechov Beit Ha-Shoeva in the Jewish Quarter. Open by prior arrangement, Sunday–Thursday for groups of twenty or more. Closed Shabbat. An entrance fee is charged. Tel. 02-628 2341.

Synagogues

Churva

This synagogue had the dubious distinction of being built in the first years of the eighteenth century by Rabbi Yehudah HaChassid, a follower of the false messiah, Shabtai Tzvi (1626–1676). The synagogue, constructed on the ruins of the Crusader Church of St. Martin, was next to the ruins of the Ramban Synagogue.

The rabbi passed away unexpectedly after his arrival in Jerusalem in 1701; his followers bickered amongst each other, the construction project floundered, and debts accrued. In 1721 Arab creditors destroyed the unfinished synagogue and its forty torah scrolls. The ruins were referred to

Churva Synagogue (during restoration)

as Churvat Rav Yehudah HaChassid, or simply "Churvah"—ruins.

After an interval of 135 years, Rabbi Shlomo Zalman Tzoref together with Moses Montefiore received an edict from the Ottoman sultan permitting the construction of a new synagogue on the ruins. Rabbi Shmuel Salant (1816–1909) was present at the laying of the cornerstone in 1856. Money was collected for the Beit Yaacov Synagogue, named after James Rothschild, whose family dedicated it in his memory. But, custom kept the name, "Churvah." Assad Effendi was the architect for the structure that was completed in 1864.

After the Arab Legion conquest of the Jewish Quarter, the building with its fourteen meter (forty-six feet) high window arches and twenty-seven meter (eighty-nine feet) dome was totally destroyed. In 1978 an arch that had supported the dome was reconstructed. Now the entire edifice is being rebuilt according to Effendi's model.

A new foundation was dug as part of the reconstruction, and traces of previous eras were found. Some remnants were judged to be from the period of the First Temple, remembering that this spot is near the Broad Wall, which delimited the city. Housing and a *mikvah* were unearthed from the period of the Second Temple. Archeologists are working on earthenware shards, some of which presumably date to the late First Temple period.

Ben Zakai

The Rabban Yochanan Ben Zakai synagogue serves today as the symbolic spiritual center of the Sephardic community, and it is there that the

Chief Sephardic Rabbi, the Rishon LeZion, ceremoniously takes office. The Ben-Zakai is named after the Second Temple sage, who reportedly studied at this spot in his *Beit Midrash*.

This is the most significant synagogue in a group of four Sephardic buildings. The others are Rabbi Istanbuli, Eliyahu Hanavi, and the Middle Synagogue.

The four synagogues were originally built in the early sixteenth century, and were reconstructed after 1967. The Sephardic Center, as these four synagogues have become known, contains material about Sephardic life in the Old City.

Adjacent to the Jewish Quarter parking lot. Adults: NIS 7, Children: NIS 5. Tours by rior reservation. Tel. 628 0592.

Ramban

In 1267 the seventy-two year old Ramban (Nachmanides) arrived in Akko, and soon thereafter journeyed to Jerusalem. He found marble arches and a pillar in ruins (later determined to be over Roman and Byzantine layers) on Mount Zion, and quickly constructed a synagogue. Several years after the death of the Ramban the synagogue was moved to a site inside the Old City walls. That synagogue continued to function until 1589, when the city's governor yielded to anti-Jewish incitement, closed the synagogue, and turned it into a warehouse. It was used for several secular purposes, then finally destroyed by the Arab Legion in 1948.

Tiferet Yisrael

This synagogue was built by Nissan Bak at the request of Rabbi Yisrael Friedman of Rizhin (1797–1850), a direct descendant of Rabbi Dov Ber, the Maggid of Mezritsh, who was the main disciple of Rabbi Yisrael ben Eliezer (1698–1760), better known as the Baal Shem Tov.

The first Chassidim to arrive in Jerusalem came after the Tsfat earthquake of 1837. In 1843 they were able to purchase the land for the Tiferet Yisrael Synagogue.

The dome was donated in part by Emperor Franz-Josef (1830–1916) of Austria in 1869, who was surprised that a roof had yet to be put on the building. The synagogue was completed in 1872.

Just as *Mitnagdim* prayed in the Churva Synagogue, Tiferet Yisrael was a Chassidic center, but prayer was not the sole purpose of the building. During the 1936–1939 Arab riots, an observation post was built on the roof. Tiferet Yisrael, a magnificent architectural landmark, was destroyed in the fighting of 1948.

Temple Institute *(See color plate 7, p. 99)*

The Temple is a central theme in Judaism and accounts for 202 of the commandments. Numerous times the Torah tells us, "Make me a Mikdash." *Machon HaMikdash* (Temple Institute) is a statement that we still must occupy ourselves with those commandments. We cannot build the Third Temple, but we must understand the worship as much as possible.

The Temple Institute is an educational project that reaches out to not only those who tour its museum. It has developed a publishing program and a proactive curriculum brought to Israeli schools to teach both religious and non-religious students about the Temple. Since Rabbi Yisrael Ariel helped found the Institute in 1987, more than one million visitors have toured its facilities.

The Institute has devoted extensive efforts to learn about the vessels and garments used in the Temple. It is not trying to duplicate the worship of the Second Temple; rather, it tries to understand the implements used and create new ones to illustrate the commandments involved.

For example, one exhibit stresses that the ritual shovel used for incense had certain qualities. The way in which it was made, however, was not absolutely strict. Artisans also had artistic license. Within Torah requirements those artisans could embellish and decorate the shovel according to their own artistic taste.

There are two different ideas concerning the *tzitz* (golden crown—one of the eight garments of the high priest). One opinion states that it contained one line of writing; another opinion says that there were two lines. Rabbi Yisroel Yaakov Fisher (1928-2003) of the *Eida* Rabbinic Court found a solution that satisfies both opinions. Was this the way that the *tzitz* looked in the time of the Temple? Perhaps not. For the Institute that is not the issue. Rather, they raised the question and arrived at an innovative solution that meets all the demands of Jewish Law.

Tractate *Ta'anit* mentions a gold plated *shofar* blown on Rosh Hashanah. It is one thing to read through a Talmud passage and imagine how it must have looked. It is quite another matter to make such a shofar. Then one must deal with issues such as thickness of the gold plating without distorting sound. One conclusion is quite obvious—only superb craftsmen could have produced the vessels used in the Temple.

The *choshen* of the high priest is a good example of the work of the Institute. What was the thread in the *choshen*? How was it dyed? The *choshen* held twelve stones, one for each Biblical tribe. Which stones were they? The Institute spent ten years and $80,000 to resolve these questions. Prominent rabbis were consulted. Some thirty different traditional methods were reviewed, from translations of the Bible into Aramaic through current rabbinic sources. Finally it was concluded that the color of the stones was probably more important than the exact type. What is paramount is that we are looking at sources, addressing issues, and learning about the Temple. We do so many things in memory of the Temple, but that is not enough. We cannot neglect learning.

Temple Institute (Machon HaMikdash), Rechov Misgav LaDach 19, Jewish Quarter, Old City. Tel. 02-626 4545.

Hours: Sunday—Thursday 0900–1700. Fridays and day before holidays: 0900–1200 (1300 in summer). Closed Shabbat.

Entrance Fee: NIS 20 (NIS 15 for children and seniors). It is recommended to take a guided tour (English is available) and not walk unescorted through the exhibits. There is an additional charge of NIS 70 if there are fewer than ten participants in a guided tour. The tour lasts approximately one hour and includes a thirty-minute film. For arrangements it is best to call in advance.

Other Sites in the Old City

Ramparts and Gates of the Old City

One way to see the gates of the Old City is to walk the exterior path that encircles the outside of the city walls. Another way is to walk the Ramparts atop then Old City walls.

Ramparts (See color plate 8, p. 99)

The Ottoman Janissaries are long gone. Jordanian snipers are past history. Now those peering down from atop the walls of the Old City are primarily tourists getting a very unique view of Jerusalem.

A walk on the walls (the area comprising the eastern and southern walls of the Temple Mount is off limits) starts at Jaffa Gate, from where one can go either towards Mt. Zion or in the direction of the Damascus Gate (more interesting of the two routes).

At the beginning of the sixteenth century the 4.2 kilometer (2.5 mile) long city walls lay in ruin, destroyed during battles of the Middle Ages. For more than two centuries following the Crusader Era, Jerusalem had been held securely by Moslem rulers, including the Mamluks, and the Ottomans. Fervor to expand Christendom, however, was sweeping Europe, as missionaries propelled the Age of Discovery that colonized the Western Hemisphere and chartered new routes to India and the Orient.

Suleiman rallied his Ottoman forces and rebuilt the walls to protect against a feared new crusade by Charles V (1500–1558) of Spain. Building started in 1535/6 and continued until 1541; the project was designed by Sinan Pasha (1506–1596), Suleiman's primary military architect. Many of the towers on the wall were never completed, after the Ottomans decided that a Christian invasion was not imminent. According to one tradition, the Ottomans dismantled Crusader-era churches and used the stones to build the walls. Thirty-five watch towers were planned (half never built), each two or three levels high to accommodate a stable, living quarters, and a look-out position.

There is considerable climbing of steps. Comfortable shoes should be worn for walking on stones, which can be slippery when wet after rains.

Jaffa (See color plate 9, p. 100)

The Jaffa Gate in Arabic is called Bab Al-Khalil, or the Hebron Gate, since the road in front of it leads to the City of the Patriarchs. In the past it was also known as the Bethlehem Gate and in the Middle Ages as David's Gate, because of the adjacent Tower of David. Until the 1870s Jaffa Gate was locked every evening at sunset.

The Jaffa Gate that was erected by Suleiman was destroyed by Christian forces, but only centuries later, when General Edmund Allenby came into the city. Remodeling of sorts came in 1949, when Jaffa Gate constituted the last Jordanian position on their side of No-Man's Land. They sealed the gate with stone and concrete. The gate was damaged in the Six Day War, then rebuilt to its early twentieth century look by the Israelis.

New

Moving to the east, the ramparts walkway comes in close proximity to the New City, then it turns towards New Gate.

At the end of the nineteenth century Europeans pressured the Ottomans to open a gate to aid Christian pilgrims in reaching the Christian Quarter without going through city streets. In 1887 the Ottomans succumbed to pressure and opened the Sultan Abdul Hamid II Gate, but the long name never caught on. Almost immediately the accepted appellation became New Gate. So it is still called today.

Even in relatively recent times life near New Gate was different from today. Dr. John Tleel (1928-   ) of the Christian Quarter recalls his family house that once stood just outside New Gate. During the 1948 fighting the Tleel's were hastily evacuated from that building in what became No-Man's Land. Tleel's father's dental office was closed. Not all is blood and guts in times of war; during one of the cease-fires Israeli and Jordanian Arab Legion soldiers co-operated to move the dental equipment inside the Old City.

Looking at the Old City from this section of the ramparts also dispels a mistaken stereotype of impoverished dwellings and substandard living. Gazing down, one can see well-kept and relatively modern buildings, and an occasional parked car. Many of the buildings on the streets from the Jaffa and Damascus Gates through the *shuk* (market place) to the Western Wall were built during the Middle Ages or reasonably soon thereafter. The buildings bordering the wall, however, were constructed during the nineteenth century and are much easier to maintain.

The architecture of the gate is relatively simplistic, and it was designed without considering its value for defensive purpose. The shops and houses just inside the Gate date to construction by the Greek Orthodox Church in the 1890s.

This gate was closed between 1948 and 1967, since it was located virtually on the Jordan-Israel cease fire line.

Damascus (See color plate 10, p. 100)

Next along the walls is the Damascus Gate. This is another gate built by Suleiman in 1538, and it still carries an inscription dedicated to the Ottoman ruler.

During the Jordanian period this gate became the primary entrance to the Old City. Jaffa Gate was closed. Damascus Gate (in Hebrew "Shechem"—Nablus—Gate) offered the best access to the mosques on the Temple Mount inside the Old City and the modern business district outside. Often the gate was blocked by taxis that could pull up virtually to the entrance. Under Israeli rule the entrance way to the Damascus Gate was renovated.

The Arabic name of the gate is "Bab El-Amud," or Gate of the Pillar. One explanation is that this is a remnant of Roman tradition. The gate was the main Roman entrance to Jerusalem, and it was the beginning of the Cardo.

Current politics sometimes obfuscate facts. Even in the twentieth century distances were measured from the "pillar" (albeit no longer existing) to other cities. Damascus is only 214 kilometers (134 miles) from Jerusalem, or only slightly farther than going from London to Birmingham, or from New York City to Philadelphia. Hence, the name, Damascus Gate, is not surprising.

From the guard station above the gate one can watch the flow of people and the market activity. The sounds of typical Middle Eastern commerce are as impressive as the sights.

The walk on the ramparts continues onward past Herod's Gate, then turns the corner opposite the Rockefeller Museum, moving onward until Lion's Gate, which is the end of the tour. Most tourists might want to exit at the Damascus Gate, since there is relatively less to see in the later section.

Remains of the Roman Gate have been unearthed under today's Damascus Gate and are open as a museum (see entry).

Flower

As with the other gates of the Old City, Flower Gate has several other names. In English it is often called Herod's Gate, based upon the mistaken Crusader notion that it led to Herod's Palace.

"Flower" Gate is derived from the floral designs sculpted on the façade of the gate.

Another name is Bab-a-Sahairad, "those who do not sleep at night," referring to a Moslem cemetery opposite the gate behind the stores on the other side of the street. (In the 1990s heavy rains caused the collapse of the cemetery retaining wall, resulting in the deaths of twenty-three people in a café adjacent to the cemetery wall.)

Lions' *(See color plate 12, p. 100)*

This is one of the gates built by Suleiman in the sixteenth century. Since the middle of the nineteenth century Jews have called this Lions Gate (Arabic, Bab al-Chutta) after the two pairs of carved lions (in fact, leopards) on the façade. This was the symbol of Baybars, the Mamluk sultan, who conquered Jerusalem in 1260.

It was through this gate that the main Israeli force entered the Old City during the Six Day War.

Mercy (Golden)

Shaar HaRachamin has been closed for centuries. It is through a gate here in the Eastern Wall of the Temple Mount that the Priest returned after burning the Red Heiffer.

There is a traditional belief that this will be the route of the Messiah to the rebuilt Third Temple. Outside the gate there is a Moslem cemetery. According to one explanation, Moslems were buried here to stop the High Priest from entering the Temple Mount, since traversing graves would defile him. Another explanation is that Moslems buried here wanted to be the first to be awoken upon the Resurrection of the Dead.

During Christian rule during the Middle Ages the gate was opened for religious purposes. After Moslems regained rule, the gate was once again sealed permanently.

Dung

An alternative Arabic name for the Dung Gate is Bab Silwan, based upon the neighborhood in the area of what was once the City of David. Silwan was populated by Yemeni Jews who immigrated to Palestine in the 1880s, but the Jewish settlement was abandoned after the riots of 1936. Previously the gate was called Bab Almaghraba after the Moghrabi neighborhood inside the city wall.

During Jordanian rule the Dung Gate was widened to accommodate cars. Several meters away there is a pedestrian passage discovered and opened in 1995 based upon ancient sources. It is the terminus of a Roman street, part of which can be seen inside the walls. For many years it was thought that Dung Gate was that passage.

In March 2007 excavations began in the "Givati Parking Lot" near Dung Gate. Initial findings in a multi-year project have yielded a multi-storey building of monumental proportion with both Byzantine and Hellenistic layers. There is evidence of wanton destruction of the earlier structure, presumably at the time of the Destruction. At this time all theories about the ownership and use of the building are pure conjecture.

Zion

The Zion Gate is basically Ottoman, but during the fighting of 1948 it was damaged. Restoration began in 2007 and was completed in 2008. Only some of the bullet holes and damage were repaired to leave others as an historical reminder of the fighting. An inscription dedicated to Sultan Suleiman can also be seen.

Remnants of the Ayyubid Gate built in 1212 by Sultan al-Malik al-Muazzam are nearby.

Hulda (See color plate 11, p. 100)

See Davidson Center entry.

Entrance to the Ramparts is from Jaffa Gate (Jaffa Gate to Jewish Quarter or Jaffa Gate to Lion's Gate) and from the Damascus Gate (to either Jaffa Gate or Lion's Gate). Open 0900–1600 with slight variation for season. Not Shomer Shabbat. Fee: Adults NIS 15, Children and Seniors NIS 8. Tel. 02-628 2341. Save the receipt for presentation upon leaving.

Tower of David *(See color plate 13, p. 101)*

The Tower of David, just inside Jerusalem's Jaffa Gate, is an excellent place to start a first-time tour of Jerusalem. The museum, opened in 1989, offers a rudimentary overview of the history of Jerusalem, and a breathtaking panoramic view of the city. An annotated map provides the context for what the visitor will later see as he wanders about Jerusalem.

The museum is designed to appeal to the widest spectrum of visitors. To the religious Jew the history of Jerusalem is not an unknown subject. Yet, even for the history buff nine unique models enrich understanding.

The first model, for example, shows the topography of Jerusalem without the clutter of buildings. It is a perfect way to understand the hills and valleys of the city.

The location of the Tower of David is strategic. Lore says that King David built a fortress there. Recent archeology on the site has uncovered parts of the Herodian-era Tower of Phasael that once guarded one of Herod's many palaces. The tower was not impregnable. It was apparently held for a month by Jewish forces during the revolt against Rome, but it then fell. In later years the Tower and accompanying citadel were rebuilt with a moat, but remember water is scarce, particularly during the hot summer months. Unlike moats in England, this one was built to be waterless, with steep and slippery walls designed to fend off invaders.

The intent of the museum is to explain history, not to display it. Hence, the exhibits are explicative. An illuminated map, for example, shows the route of the water system during the period of Hezkiyahu the King. A miniature reconstruction gives a very vivid depiction of the Second Temple and of what has come to be called Robinson's Arch.

Jerusalem was conquered at different times by different nations. One display is the Medieval Islamic era, taking into consideration religious sensitivities. Both Jews and Arabs flourished in Jerusalem, as soldiers fought off Christian invaders from Europe. Until the retreat of the Jordanians from Jerusalem in 1967, the Tower of David was used for centuries as a fort of Moslem troops, except during the British Mandate. When the museum was built, the mosque in the building was left intact out of religious respect.

The tour of the museum is chronological, always with a time scale, so that the visitor knows exactly what period is being explained. Some of the metal models show development of the city—the Lower City in the time of the First Temple, the exaggerated Third Wall that typified Herod's mania to build. One model, however, is not newly made by museum authorities.

In 1864 Stefan Illes, a priest and bookbinder, came to Jerusalem from Pressburg (Bratislava). Soon he began to build an extraordinary model of Jerusalem in his day. It was eventually put on display at the 1873 Vienna Universal Exhibition in the Ottoman Pavilion. For many years it was "lost," then rediscovered in 1984, restored, and put on display. The 1:500 model was done in exact detail, with one exception. This was an Ottoman project. The mosque minarets were imposingly high, well out of their true proportion. That model is down a flight of steps near the end of the tour of the museum.

Next to the Illes recreation there is a collection of dolls illustrating typical Jerusalem characters. Even the ultra-orthodox are represented.

For various reasons it was decided to stop the chronology of history in the museum in 1948. Other museums in Jerusalem cover the years since then.

The Tower of David is highly recommended with a guided tour arranged in advance (specify that a religious tour is requested). Allot between ninety and 120 minutes.

Entrance: Adults NIS 30, children NIS 15. Special exhibits involve an additional fee. Sunday–Thursday 1000–1600. Closed Friday. Not Shomer Shabbat. Guided tours in English, Sunday–Thursday at 1100; included in entrance fee. Tel. 02-626 5327.

Zedekiah's Cave

This cave, rediscovered in the 1850s after centuries of neglect, derives its name from a chapter in ancient history. It is clear from expert opinion that the 225 meter-long (738 feet) cave was a quarry, and there is a traditional belief that stones for the First Temple were taken from here.

Yosef Ben-Matityahu, usually referred to as Josephus (37 CE – c. 100 CE), mentions this cave in his description of the Herodian Third Wall. He refers to it as the Quarry of the Kings.

During the British Mandate stones were taken from the cave and used to build the clock tower above Jaffa Gate. That tower was destroyed before the establishment of the State of Israel.

Zedekiah's Cave is a short walk to the east of Damascus Gate. Hours are Sunday–Thursday 0900–1600 (winter)/1700 (summer). Holiday eve until 1400. Entrance fee: Adults NIS 16, Children and Seniors NIS 10. Comfortable walking shoes are highly recommended.

Zedekiah's Cave. Was an ancient quarry (Sheina)

Mount of Olives

Graves of Prophets

Burial in caves was considered an honor during Biblical and Talmudic times. This is unlike Roman catacombs, which were used for the indigent. Perhaps the best preserved burial cave is on the upper slope of the Mount of Olives, where Haggai, Malachi, and Zechariah are buried.

An official sign marks an entrance into a courtyard, in the center of which a stone staircase leads down into the hand-carved cave. A hole in the ceiling sheds light into the cave, which is naturally cool even on the hottest of summer days.

The outer wall of the cave contains fifty burial niches arranged in a semi-circle, except for a small room that houses several burial slots. A parallel inner semi-circle contains no graves. One explanation is that the inner passage was used for prayer. This seems rather dubious, since there is no Jewish prohibition to pray next to a grave. To the contrary, there has been a centuries-old tradition to offer prayers in close proximity to graves. More plausibly, the inner semi-circle was planned for later use, which never happened.

The cave was sold to the Russian Orthodox Church in 1883 despite vociferous Jewish objection and a letter of restraint issued by the Ottoman sultan. The church, operating through the Russian counsel, said that it wanted the cave for "scientific" reasons. They promised not to build a church or place religious symbols in the area.

For five decades the cave was administrated by the Othman family, Moslems who had lived in the Lifta-Romema area in West Jerusalem until they fled in 1948. They found refuge on the Mount of Olives, where for six months they slept in the cave. At that time the only building in the area was a small shed that stood near the cave. The Othmans made a deal with the Russian Orthodox Church; they were permitted to build houses and live on the cemetery in exchange for taking care of the cave.

During the period of Jordanian rule Christian pilgrims to Jerusalem visited sites on the lower sections of the mountain, but the Graves of the Prophets were not on the standard tourist route. That, however, began to change soon after the Six Day War. A representative of the Israel Ministry of Religious Affairs visited the Othman family and reached a formal agreement. In exchange for payment from the Ministry, the head of the household became responsible for keeping the site ready for tourists. (That agreement officially expired with the death of Mr. Othman some ten years later, but it was continued informally for more than twenty years.)

A visit to the Graves of the Prophets yields good insight into burial in the period of the Second Temple, and no one can doubt the religious value of praying next to the graves of prophets.

The Graves are not serviced by Israeli public transportation. To reach the Graves of the Prophets, travel by car to the Seven Arches Hotel on the Mount of Olives. As you face the Old City, there is a staircase to the right. Walk down about three or four meters (twelve to fifteen feet). The entrance to the cave area is to the left.

The arrangement with the Othman family to provide tours has been discontinued. The tours are now being given Monday–Thursday, 0900–1500 by a church representative. Even though the guide tries to refrain from introducing religious content, a tour under these circumstances is not recommended. If you want to see the cave, do it by private guide (coordinated with the church representative).

Kidron Valley

The Kidron Valley lies between the Mount of Olives and the Temple Mount. In ancient times it was a frequently used burial area. The most important ancient graves in the Kidron Valley are those of Absalom and Josaphat.

Kidron Valley. Grave of the Ben Ish Chai

Mount Zion

Cable Car Museum *(See color plate 14, p. 101)*

When the British departed Mandate Palestine, they essentially left both Jews and Arabs to fend for themselves. Each side tried to defend the territory already held and take additional turf. One strategic point was Mount Zion, which the Harel Brigade of the Palmach captured on 18 May 1948 as part of a broader campaign to break the siege on the Jewish Quarter. The Jewish Quarter was lost, but Jewish forces retained their foothold on Mount Zion. The question became how to bring supplies to Mount Zion without being exposed to Arab gunfire and without trekking up or down the mountain. Initially a narrow tunnel connected Mount Zion with Yemin Moshe, but the restricted width was cumbersome, and the steep incline was difficult.

In December 1948 Uriel Hefetz, later to serve as a senior officer in the IDF Engineering Corps, proposed a steel cable 200 meters (650 feet) in length and suspended fifty meters (165 feet) above the Valley of Hinnon. Cars making the trip in two minutes each held a maximum weight of 250 kilograms. (550 pounds). One end of the cable was on Mount Zion; the other end was in the abandoned St. John's Ophthalmic Hospital on Derech Hebron just below Yemin Moshe. For six months the cable was raised at night then lowered before daybreak, so the operation would go undetected. Until 1972 the cable car was kept in readiness in case its operation would once again become necessary. Recently the operations room and one of the cars have become a museum.

What happened to the hospital that stood at the site? It was established in 1882 at the initiative of the Duke of Kent, and for many years it served as the only eye hospital in Ottoman Palestine. *Gratis* care was given to all regardless of creed. World War I caused the hospital to cease normal operations, as Ottoman forces used the basement as a weapons arsenal, but under British rule the hospital resumed normal work and was even expanded with southern and western annexes.

The western wing across the street was designed in Romantic style by Clifford Holliday (1897–1960) and dedicated by Lord Allenby in 1927. An underground tunnel connects the two parts of the former hospital. Today the western annex houses the Jerusalem House of Quality—an art gallery and studios.

In the midst of the War of Independence the Order of St. John transferred operations to a building in Khan al-Zeitun, a large, covered market in the Moslem Quarter leading to the Temple Mount. The former hospital was initially used by the IDF, but in 1964 the buildings were sold to private investors. At one point a yeshiva was located in part of the building.

On 5 March 1959 St. John's laid the cornerstone for a new, large hospital in the Arab neighborhood of Sheikh Jarrah, and in the following year the forty-nine-bed institution was dedicated by King Hussein. Today the ophthalmic hospital provides services ranging from eyeglass prescriptions to eye surgery and offers twenty-four-hour emergency services.

Derech Hebron 15. Open Sunday–Thursday 0900-1600, Friday 0900–1400. Entrance fee: gratis. Tel. 02-627 7550. Fax: 02-627 7962. When facing the Mount Zion Hotel, the entrance is at the far left of the building. There also is passage to the museum from the fifth floor of the hotel. This is included in Mt. Zion, since that was the destination of the cable car.

Holocaust Museum *(See color plate 15, p. 101)*

Today there is an increasing number of Holocaust museums and memorials throughout the world, but the Chamber of the Holocaust on Mt. Zion is unique. The facility is more than fifty years old, established by war survivors who wanted others never to forget what had happened. The objective is to show how Jews kept the Torah and its commandments despite Nazi atrocities.

A shofar, reportedly blown in the Bergen-Belsen concentration camp despite the dangers inherent in such an act is at the entrance to the museum. The person blowing it was summarily put to death by Nazi officers.

Pages of a handwritten prayerbook were also recovered from a concentration camp. A prisoner had committed to writing those prayers that he could remember. He did not have clean sheets of paper, so he used the back-sides of scrap paper.

There is a bloodstained Torah scroll from Wengrow, Poland, once a Torah center and on the eve of World War II home to slightly more than 5000 Jews. The Nazis stabbed the rabbi of the town in the back. His retort was defiant, "May my death be considered sanctification of G-d's name!" The blood on the Torah scroll is probably that of the rabbi.

The museum has soap made from the bodies of Jews. (Since the Chamber of the Holocaust is maintained by the Diaspora Yeshiva, there is strict respect to Jewish Law. The head of the *yeshiva* consulted Rabbi Eliashiv, who decided that the soap and bloodstained Torah do not constitute *tum'at ha-ohel*; Cohanim may enter the building.)

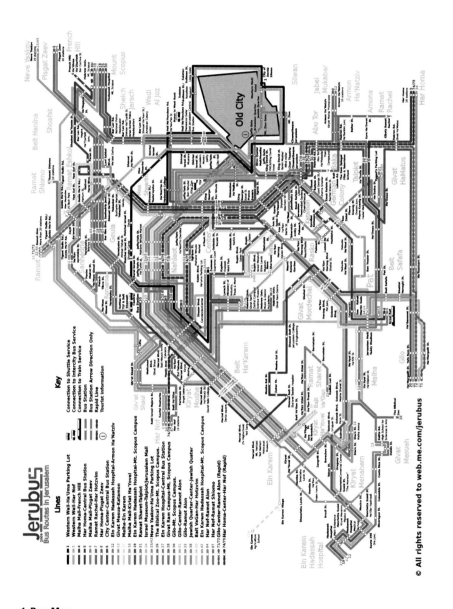

1-Bus Map

2. (above) Temple Mount. From the Mount of Olives *(See p. 51)*
3. (below left) Western Wall Tunnel © *(See p. 53)*
4. (below right) Chain of Generations © *(See p. 55)*

**5. (above) Western Wall.
Praying at the Kotel.**
(See p. 57)

6. (above left) View of the Cardo (Sheina)
(See p. 72)
**7. (above right) Menorah made by Temple
Institute experts** *(See p. 82)*

In left:
8. Along the Ramparts *(See p. 85)*

9. (left) Jaffa Gate
(See p. 86)
10. (below left):
Damascus Gate
(Sheina) *(See p. 87)*

11. (below right)
Hulda Gates to the
Temple Mount.
Once a primary
entrance, but
sealed for centuries
(See p. 89)

12. Lions Gate. Named after the decorative lions. In 1967 Israeli forces entered the
Old City from here *(See p. 88)*

13. (top) Tower of David. Next to Jaffa Gate *(See p. 89)*

14. (left): Cable car. Used by IDF to Mount Zion (Sheina) *(See p. 95)*

15. (left) Holocaust Museum on Mount Zion. Tombstones symbolizing destroyed communities *(See p. 96)*

16. King David. Tomb on Mount Zion. *(See p. 113)*

17. (top left) British Military Cemetery on Mt. Scopus. Graves of Jewish WWI soldiers (Sheina) *(See p. 115)*
18. (top right) Grave of Nicanor. In the Hebrew University Mount Scopus Botanical Gardens *(See p. 116)*
19. (left): Model depicting te battle for Ammunition Hill during the Six Day War *(See p. 120)*
20. (below) Belz Torah Center *(See p. 125)*

21. (top left) Bible Lands Museum. Door lintel of a synagogue, probably from the Golan, ca. 300 – 600 C.E. © *(See p. 128)*

22. (top right) Bloomfield Science Museum © *(See p. 131)*

23. (left) Guela. Kikar Shabbat (entrance to Geula) *(See p. 138)*

24. (below) Biblical Givat Shaul. King Hussein's unfinished palace (where goats roam freely) (Sheina) *(See p. 139)*

25. (left) Great Synagogue. Mezuzah collection in the entrance hallway *(See p. 141)*

26. Gush Katif Museum- Before and after Disengagement © *(See p. 164)*

(right) after (below) before

27. (left) Grave of
HaRav Shlomo Zalman
Auerbach (1910-1995)
on Har Hamenuchot
Cemetery *(See p. 144)*

28. (below) Har Hame-
nuchot. Grave of the
Chida (See p. 144)

29. (top) Israel Museum. Miniature of Jerusalem during Second Temple Period *(See p. 150)*

30. (right) Italian Jewry Museum *(See p. 153)*

31. (below) Knesset *(See p. 155)*

32. (left) Machne Yehuda. Sun dail on Zohorei Hama Synagogue *(See p. 156)*

33. (above) Mea Shearim *(See p. 159)*

34. (right) Motza. Renovated synagogue *(See p. 161)*

35. (left) Museum on the Seam. In the confusion of war © *(See p. 162)*

36. (left) North African Jewry. © *(See p. 164)*

37. (right) Otzar HaPoskim. Library *(See p. 165)*

38. (below) Rav Kook's House. The study *(See p. 167)*

39. (left and below right) Rebbe's Museum. *(See p. 169)*

40. (below) Supreme Court *(See p. 179)*

41. (top left and right) Ticho House. From the collection on Chanukah menorahs *(See p. 179)*

42. (right) Third Wall. Note stones to the right of the steps *(See p. 180)*

43. (left) Tomb of the Kings *(See p. 182)*

**44. (left) Yad Ben Zvi.
From the library collection
(Sheina)** *(See p. 183)*

**45. (below) Zichron Moshe.
Former Lamel School in the
neighborhood** *(See p. 188)*

There are times when Jews make extraordinary efforts to keep a mitz-vah. A Chanukah menorah made from potato peels comes from Auschwitz. The wicks are threads from clothing.

Graphic pictures donated by the son of a soldier who was part of the force that liberated Buchenwald stand testimony to the cruelty of the Nazis.

Several of the walls of the Chamber of the Holocaust have grave-like stones, in memorial to the many Jewish communities obliterated without cemeteries where the dead can be mourned. Those stones were put in place by survivors. If there are no graves, at least the stones will stand as a perma-nent reminder of six million Jews who were ruthlessly slaughtered.

The Nazis strove not only to exterminate the Jewish people; they waged war on the Torah itself, trying to wipe out basic religious values. The Nazis tried to desecrate the Torah in every way possible. There are nu-merous items made from the parchment of Torah scrolls—soles of shoes, drums, handbags and satchels. There is even a "shirt" showing *Haazinu* and possibly worn as a mock garment at a ball.

Mt. Zion. Bus No. 38 or a ten–fifteen minute walk from either the Western Wall (steep incline) or Jaffa Gate (easier). Open Sunday–Thursday 0900–1545, Friday 0900–1330. Closed Shabbat. NIS 12 fee. Tours in Eng-lish by prior arrangement—Tel. 02-671 5105.

King David's Tomb *(See color plate 16, p. 102)*

For many years the grave of King David on Mount Zion has been a point of prayer for Jews.

Benjamin of Tudela (twelveth century) relates that in his time Jews and other non-Moslems were denied entrance to the Tomb of David. Dur-ing the British Mandate the restriction was eased; Jewish prayer was permit-ted on Shavuot, the Yahrzeit of the Biblical king. In the subsequent War of Independence, Jewish forces tried and failed to capture the Jewish Quarter just inside Zion Gate. The gate was sealed. Mount Zion fell under Jewish control with access using a path from the railroad station. There was no longer a prohibition for Jews to pray. This became the closest point to the Temple Mount. Despite a tense atmosphere Jews came in large numbers to pray next to the Tomb. Approaching any nearer to the Old City was forbid-den due to fear of sniper fire.

Just as today, in the period of the First Temple Mount Zion was outside the walls of the Old City. During the reign of King David, Mount Zion was in all probability an area of woods and fields with no buildings or roads.

There are those who have tried to cast doubt on the veracity of the burial location. I Kings 2:10 records that King David was buried in the

"City of David." There is no contradiction. Burial was never permitted inside city walls due to laws of ritual purity. Most plausibly the burial area on Mount Zion was considered part of the City of David for the purpose of internment, even though it was beyond the city wall. According to tradition and confirmed by the *Ari*, it was on Mount Zion that King David is buried.

As history unfolded, non-Jews attached importance to the site of the Biblical grave. Christians, in particular, assigned historical significance to the area. For that reason the building now standing over the grave is a Crusader structure built in Gothic style in 1335.

Sometimes unfortunate events provide positive opportunities. During 1948 fighting, a mortar shell struck the site. Jacob Pinkerfeld (died 23 September 1956 in sniper fire from across the Green Line), an Israeli architect and archeologist, was dispatched to inspect the damage and insure that repairs would not destroy important artifacts. His professional specialty melded together both of his pursuits; he was a recognized expert in both the architecture and archeology of historic synagogues. Pinkerfeld inspected the building, which only because of the mortar's damage could be done without causing a religious furor.

Pinkerfeld lifted the marble floor slabs and was able to discover three earlier levels. First, he uncovered a twelveth-century Crusader floor. Still further down the archeologist unearthed a Byzantine mosaic floor probably built during the fifth or sixth centuries. Yet lower were the foundation remains of Roman-era construction. Pinkerfeld casts doubt about the authenticity of the site, yet at the very same time he recognizes its importance to what he determines to have been a first century CE building for prayer.

Today there is a huge black granite stone covered in cloth in the Tomb of David. That is not a sarcophagus holding human remains; it is a covering to the entrance of the cave where King David is buried.

Mount Scopus

Augusta Victoria Hospital

Today this building, just south of the university, is a hospital run by the Lutheran Church, with a church on premises. In 1898, Kaiser Wilhelm II (1859–1941) of Germany built this as a hostel for pilgrims and named it Augusta Victoria, after his wife (1858–1921). Following the declaration of British rule, the new High Commissioner renovated the building and used it as his residence. In 1927, however, an earthquake damaged the building, and the High Commissioner moved to Jebel Mukabir (today's Armon HaNatziv). Augusta Victoria then became a hospital.

British Cemetery *(See color plate 17, p. 103)*

This is a World War I burial ground for fallen soldiers and a memorial for the 900 soldiers for whom there are no graves. There is a basic monotony in gazing at some 2400 standard military tombstones, but at closer look twenty-four of the stones near the northern perimeter fence are different. They are decorated with a Jewish star, and they mark the burial of Jewish soldiers. There are another nineteen graves that are also different. Sixteen of these belong to German soldiers killed in battle, and three mark the burial of Ottoman troops.

The British government is insistent that there be no special treatment of deceased soldiers because of race, religion, or rank. AJEX (Association of Jewish Ex-Servicemen) is a private organization headquartered in London that arranges for prayers next to Jewish graves.

There are five other British military cemeteries in what was Mandate Palestine. The largest, with 6000 graves, is in Ramleh, and others are located in Beersheba, Haifa, and Gaza. Jews are amongst the 15,980 British soldiers buried in these cemeteries. A lesser known cemetery is on Rechov Korei HaDorot in the Talpiyot section of Jerusalem, where forty-seven Hindu, Sikh and Gurka soldiers are buried; there are also Indian Muslim graves and a mass grave for about 290 Turks who fought against the British.

The cemeteries in Jerusalem, Beersheba and Haifa are open daily and can be visited during daylight hours. The cemetery in Ramleh closes at 2 p.m. Run by the British Government. No fee.

University

The Hebrew University of Jerusalem was founded as a secular institution, and it remains such; yet, there always has been religious input. Rabbis were present at the opening ceremony on 1 April 1925. This first university in Mandate Palestine is an integral part of Israeli history.

The university occupies a large tract of land purchased in large part with monies raised by *Chovevei Tziyon*. The land, however, was not totally empty when it was acquired.

In 1902 Sir John Gray Hill, a wealthy English lawyer, built a house on the land overlooking Jerusalem in one direction and the Dead Sea in the other. He had traveled to Palestine every year since 1887, and in 1889 he bought the land in question. The view was magnificent, but thirteen years went by before Gray Hill and his wife decided to build. Lady Caroline Emily Gray Hill (1843–1924) was an artist, and this was by all measures an ideal location for her studio. As one visitor later described the view from the house, it was a "vision of beauty."

During construction of the house, however, something totally unexpected occurred. Workers found an ancient cave. The area was excavated, and an important discovery was made—ossuaries with bones and jewels. There was no question to whom the burial area belonged; written are the words, "Nicanor from Alexandria." *(See color plate 18, p. 103)*

As the Talmud (*Yoma* 38a) describes, Nicanor traveled from Alexandria to bring gates for the Second Temple. He loaded two bronze gates on a ship, but a large wave threatened the vessel. Nicanor cast one gate overboard, but the sea continued to rage. Then, he declared that he should be thrown into the sea with the second gate. Suddenly, the sea became calm. By a miracle the first gate appeared when the ship arrived in Akko. Some said that a sea monster spit it out. Others claim that the bronze gate became attached to the underside of the ship. In any event, the Gates of Nicanor were installed on the western side of the Women's Section in the Second Temple. Eventually, gold-colored gates were put on all of the entrances to recall this miracle.

By the accounts of Josephus, the gates were truly impressive. Estimates are that they stood forty cubits wide and fifty cubits high.

In the case of this grave do not start looking for the burial coffin in the closed-off cave. Archeologists carted it off to London years ago.

In 1914 the Gray Hill House was sold to the builders of the Hebrew University, and the area was totally redeveloped. The burial cave of Nicanor, though, was not destroyed.

In 1926 land with the burial cave was allocated for the Botanical Gardens at Hebrew University. Professors Alexander Eig (1894–1938) and

Otto Warburg (1859–1938) of the Botany Department were in charge of the project. Eig had immigrated to Palestine and is renowned for discovering several different plants. He was interested in the flora of Palestine. Warburg was an early Zionist who made significant contributions to agriculture in Palestine. Planting of the Botanical Gardens began in 1931, and today it contains some 950 species in twenty-five dunams (6.2 acres).

Over the years the academic programs of the university grew. From three departments, each housed in a separate building, new subjects were added. More buildings were constructed. An amphitheater was built for ceremonies. Even lions were brought to the university. Real ones! They were part of what became the Biblical Zoo (see entry).

Not everything in the history of Hebrew University was honest! In the 1930s the university was a knowing accomplice of bogus academic certificates! The university had started as a graduate school, and only later were undergraduate studies added. Mandate officials were strictly enforcing immigration restrictions for Jews trying to flee Hitler's Germany. A loophole was education. So, Hebrew University knowingly recognized forged academic records to allow German Jews to enter.

At 0945 on 13 April 1948 history stopped. A convoy of ten vehicles bound for the university and Hadassah Hospital was attacked in Sheikh Jarrah, opposite today's Kenyon School of Archeology and only minutes by foot from a Mandate police facility (later to become the Shepherd Hotel during the Jordanian period). A large monument marks the site of the attack. Five vehicles escaped, but in the remaining five, seventy-eight Jews were murdered. It was eminently clear that life on Mount Scopus had changed. Under the armistice of 1949, the Hadassah-Hebrew University complex on Mount Scopus became an Israeli enclave, accessible by escorted convoy once every two weeks. The university moved to downtown Jerusalem, then to Givat Ram.

Chanukah is a sample of Jewish resistance. From the early 1950s Israeli forces lit a large Chanukah menorah on Mt. Scopus every night of the holiday. The flames could be seen in many parts of Arab and Jewish Jerusalem. After the area was recaptured in 1967, a large Chanukah menorah was placed atop the university's Hecht Synagogue. The tradition continued.

From 1948 the entire university fell into neglect, as the IDF took control of the Mt. Scopus enclave. While Mt. Scopus was surrounded by Jordanian Jerusalem, caring for the botanical gardens was the last thing on anyone's mind. In 1967, after the Six Day War, what had been the botanical garden was in a shambles. As botanists toiled to restore the gardens, a new discovery was again made. There was another burial cave next to Nicanor!

Per inscriptions in Aramaic, the second cave contains the remains of Chananya ben Yonatan the Nazarite, his wife and family; they are interred in two sarcophaguses and fourteen ossuaries. Seeing the grave emphasizes that *nazir* is more than a technical concept in the Talmud.

Entrance to the Botanical Gardens showing the flora of Palestine and the area of the Nicanor and Nazir burial caves is *gratis*. In the Botanical Gardens, floral names are in both Hebrew and Latin.

A major attraction at the university is the aforementioned Hecht synagogue, which is in the Humanities Building. It provides a fantastic panoramic view of the Old City and its surrounding area.

When one thinks of a university, what often comes to mind is the esoteric and the theoretical. At Hebrew University many very practical items have also been produced. One development is the writing of a computerized catalogue system used by many major libraries in the world. One of its advantages is the ability to work in non-Latin languages such as Hebrew, Arabic, Russian, and even Japanese and Chinese.

Another invention developed at Hebrew University is dripped water irrigation, in which thin pipes are directed by computer to provide plants with water and nutrients according to a pre-determined schedule. The system can even be programmed so that each individual plant is given its own "recipe" and quantity. One of the major benefits is the more efficient use of water. Israeli-owned factories produce these pipes in Israel, the United States and Australia.

Hebrew University can be reached by busses 4A, 19, 26, 28, 30, and 42. Tours are by prior arrangement with the Office of the Spokesman. The Botanical Gardens are open Sunday–Thursday 0800-dusk. Closed Shabbat. Guided tours are available Tuesdays at 1100 with prior notice. Tel. 02-588 1641.

Official identity (passport or identity card preferred) is required for entrance to the campus.

Hadassah Hospital, adjacent to the university, has a small exhibit (Hebrew and English captions) about Henrietta Szold (1860–1945), who founded Hadassah in 1912. The exhibit is near the cafeteria. At the main hospital entrance go down one flight, then turn right and follow the sign.

New City

Agnon House

Shmuel Yosef Agnon (1887–1970) was the son of a rabbi who also dealt in furs. He was born in Galicia (today the Ukraine), and at the age of twenty-one immigrated to Palestine. Born with the family name, "Czaczkes," he assumed the Hebrew pseudonym, "Agnon," based upon a short story that he wrote about *"agunot"* (women left without a divorce and forbidden to remarry).

Agnon moved back to Germany in 1912 to broaden his education and taught Hebrew to earn money. He married one of his students despite her parents' objections to having a writer in the family. He was befriended by Salman Schocken (1877–1959), later to become a noted publisher, whom he met in Berlin during World War I. Schocken became the sole publisher of his books. One manuscript that Agnon wrote was never published; the virtually complete novel was destroyed in a fire in Agnon's residence in 1924. Stunned by the loss of his work and his entire library, Agnon decided to return to Palestine. His family followed him a year later.

Tragedy again struck Agnon's library in 1929, when his rented house was wrecked during the Arab riots. His family was staying with relatives in Haifa; he fled, seeking safety in the center of Jerusalem.

The house that is now a museum was designed by Fritz Korenberg in the *bauhaus* style with characteristics almost like a fortress, much to the distaste of Agnon, but certainly understandable for security reasons. That house remained his residence for the rest of his life.

Agnon's lifestyle in his Jerusalem home was autocratic and nurtured family bitterness. His upper-storey workroom was off limits to others. He would lower manuscripts in his crimped handwriting to his wife, and then retrieve them after typing. That workroom, including Agnon's book collection, is now part of the museum.

Oddly, more of Agnon's novels were published posthumously than during his lifetime. His themes were almost without exception Jewish, and he demonstrated a remarkable mastery of Biblical and Rabbinic Hebrew, as well as Midrashic literature.

The peak of Agnon's achievements was sharing the Nobel Prize for literature with Nelly Sachs (1891–1970) in 1966.

Agnon is buried on the Mount of Olives, but his legacy lives on. His works have been translated into more than forty languages, including Chinese and Arabic. The City of Jerusalem bought Agnon's house in 1970 and slowly turned it into a museum. In 2007–2008 renovations were made to restore the building to the way it was during Agnon's lifetime.

Rechov Klausner 16, Talpiyot. Open Sunday–Thursday 0900–1500; Friday and eves of holidays 0900–1300. Closed Shabbat. Bus No. 7. Entrance fee: Adults NIS 20, Children/Seniors NIS 15. Forty minute audio tape (Hebrew, English) available at no extra charge. Tel. 02-671 6498. Not handicapped accessible.

Ammunition Hill *(See color plate 19, p. 103)*

Ammunition Hill. A key battle to capture Jerusalem

All too often even the most famous lessons learnt are never applied and are quickly forgotten. The renowned Maginot Line, named after French Minister of Defense André Maginot (1877–1932), has been accepted in history as a fixed defense position that the Nazi army circumvented in its invasion of France. Some apologists have claimed that the defense deployment served its purpose by diverting an enemy attack, but the bottom line was clear—France fell.

Jordanian defenses on Ammunition Hill, then facing Jerusalem's No-Man's Land was a repeat of the same basic thinking of heavily fortified defenses and fixed-point artillery to thwart a head-on attack from the Shmuel HaNavi neighborhood. Again, mobile tactics neutralized the artillery.

The major attack on Ammunition Hill was by paratroopers who were not anticipated by Jordanians. They were backed up by Israeli ground forces that had broken Jordanian lines in a four-pronged attack in the area of Maaleh HaChamisha-Mevasseret. They plowed their way to Nablus Road and attacked from behind; the troops also connected with the isolated Israeli enclave on Mt. Scopus. Israeli soldiers proceeded several hundred meters further south to hold the conquered Ammunition Hill position.

The purpose of capturing Ammunition Hill was to prevent Jordanian soldiers from over-running the Israeli position on Mt. Scopus and to ready the way to capture the Old City. The hill dominated the Wadi Joz road to the Palestine Archeological Museum and Nablus Road to the Damascus Gate.

The attack on Ammunition Hill started just after 0200 on 6 June 1967. In all thirty-six Israelis lost their lives. Soon after daybreak the Hill and the adjoining Police School were in IDF hands. Why Ammunition Hill? The name is a left-over from Mandate days and the 1930s, when this was an ammunition storage base for the Police School.

Today the Maginot Line is remembered by a few remnants left over from a decaying relic of history that people rush to forget. Ammunition Hill, though, has been carefully maintained. It was turned into a memorial in 1975 for the 182 Israeli soldiers who fell in the battle for Jerusalem. A "Golden Wall" with their names makes certain that their memory will never be forgotten.

The museum displays pictures of the divided city and the subsequent battle. There is also an explanation in fine detail about the fight for the city and a collection of the equipment carried by Israeli troopers. If nothing else, the display humanizes soldiers, many of whom never returned home again.

The soldiers who fought at Ammunition Hill were not men of steel. Many wrote farewell letters to their families, and placed the papers in their pocket. One soldier featured in the museum recalls how he delivered two of those farewell letters to families of friends who fell in the fight for Jerusalem.

Objectively, the maps in the museum plotting the fighting for Jerusalem are most suitable for military tacticians. A more popular approach to explaining the battle for Ammunition Hill is an audio-visual presentation (English available upon request), which places Ammunition Hill in the general context of the Six Day War.

The main Jordanian underground bunker was destroyed during the fighting, but part of the trench network remains and is open to visitors. The battlefield is also explained with signs. A visit during inclement weather is not recommended, since it precludes walking through the trenches.

A library (*gratis* use) in an adjoining building houses a collection about the history of Jerusalem. The books are more or less standard, but convenient to find in one place. There is a good collection of notebooks with interesting pamphlets, new articles, and papers covering a variety of subjects from Jerusalem under Jordanian rule to various sites in Israel. Use of the library is best arranged in advance with the chief librarian.

Rechov Shragai 5. Museum is open Sunday–Thursday 0900–1700 (1800 in the summer); Friday and eves of holidays 0900–1300 (1400 in the summer). Closed Shabbat. Adults NIS 15, Youth/Students/Seniors NIS 12. Tel. 02-582 8442. Library is open Monday–Thursday 0900–1500. Busses 8, 19, 25, 26.

Bank of Israel

The Visitors' Reception area at the Bank of Israel contains an interactive exhibit explaining Israel monetary policy aimed at currency stability and detailing the history of money in the Land of Israel.

In early history "money" consisted of metal and jewelry, weighed to determine value. Only during the Persian Period were coins minted in Gaza, Ashkelon, Samaria and Jerusalem. It was during the reign of John Hycranus (High priest 135 B.C.E-104 B.C.E that Jewish motifs were first introduced on coins. (A stone mold for making coins is displayed.)

A governing principle of the Bank of Israel is that currency is a representation of nationalism. Therefore, the Bank of Israel has consistently used the Jewish motifs of ancient coins on modern coins.

During the Herodian period coins with Jewish motifs were minted in Caesarea and Jerusalem, but then Jewish motifs came to an end. After the Revolt and the Destruction, Rome dominated. The portraits of Caesars became common.

Over the following years various governments issued their own coins. The Ottomans, for example, preferred the "tughra," the symbol of the Empire.

The period of modern currency begins with the Palestine Mandate in 1917. There was no "Palestine currency" for ten years. Instead, the British introduced the Egyptian Pound as legal tender in Palestine and the Trans-Jordan (remembering that Egypt was under British military occupation at the time). Only on 1 November 1927 did the Palestine Currency Board introduce banknote denominations of 500 mils (£P½), and £P1, £P5, £P10, £P50 and £P100. This series remained throughout the Mandate, only with changes of dates and signatures of Board members (twenty-two denomination/date combinations).

During World War II the British were worried that war conditions might interrupt the supply of bank notes in Palestine. They contracted with Michael and Emil Pikovsky, Jerusalem printers, to make plates for paper bills in the denominations of £P0.050, £P0.100, £P1.000 and £P50.00.

The Pinkovsky Printing Works were well known to the British; Pinkovsky was already producing passports for the Mandate Government. (After the War Pinkovsky also printed passports and authenticating cachets for the Haganah.) The notes were not needed, and destroyed in 1945. Only specimen proofs remained and are on display at the Bank of Israel.

After independence in 1948 Israel was in immediate need of currency. Coins were out of the question. There was a scarcity of metal. So paper was issued in even extremely small denominations to fill the void. The first regular coin series began to appear only in 1949, although an improvised £ 0.025 coin appeared earlier.

Issuing currency meant making decisions. On 18 August 1948, for example, £1 notes were issued under the authority of the Anglo-Palestine Bank. On 9 June 1952 a replacement note was issued, this time under the authority of the Bank Leumi Le-Israel. Only on 27 October 1955 were the first Bank of Israel notes circulated.

The choice of pictures on currency has always been a controversial subject, and not surprisingly, it has traditionally been decided upon by committee. The first Bank of Israel notes displayed symbolic pictures of population stereotypes (pioneers, scientists, etc.) and a complicated graphic design to thwart counterfeiting. Since the third series of notes in 1972 significant personages in Jewish history have appeared on the currency.

A decision was taken in December 2009 to change all notes in about two years. The new bills will feature Israel's first prime minister, David Ben-Gurion; Zionist visionary Theodor Herzl; and former Prime Ministers Menachem Begin and Yitzhak Rabin.

The Bank is opposite the Prime Minister's Office in the Government complex. For the Visitors' Center call Tel. 02-655 2828. Visits are by group only and arranged in advance. The Visitors' Center does combine visitors into groups whenever. There is no entrance fee. A passport or other official identification document is required.

There were 1000 of these mils in one £ 1. This coin was issued on 25 October 1950 and is based upon a coin from the period of Alexander Jannaeus (103–76 BCE).

Begin Heritage Center

Begin Center. Picture of the late Prime Minister

Menachem Begin (1913-1992) was an enigmatic politician, who rose from a freedom fighter in Palestine to Prime Minister of Israel. The Begin Heritage Center in Jerusalem is dedicated to preserving the memory of his achievements.

Perhaps the most telling description of Begin was in a *précis* of his intentions that he offered upon assuming the job of prime minister. Asked what his general approach would be heading the Israeli government, Begin stated in his usual direct manner, "I want to be a Jewish prime minister!" And, that he was.

Harry Hurwitz (1924–2008), a long time Begin associate who founded and headed the Center until his death in 2008, related a story in which every Saturday night following the conclusion of the Shabbat, a small group of people would gather in the prime minister's residence for a lesson in Weekly Torah Portion. On one occasion an assistant entered with what he thought was an urgent message. U.S. President Carter was on the telephone. The religiously observant prime minister's response surprised the assistant, "Please, tell him to call back in two hours. I am now busy studying the Bible." Although Begin has passed on, the weekly lesson (in Hebrew) continues, though now on Thursday evenings in the Begin Center. There are three hundred fifty spaces, almost all open to the public by prior reservation.

In the Center there is a seventy-five minute multi-media tour offered in Hebrew and English, taking the visitor through some of the major events in Begin's life. This is not a critical assessment of Begin's contribution to history; it is a determined effort to project Begin in the image seen by his followers. The multi-media presentation is extremely effective, utilizing film, sound, stills, and museum-style exhibits to convey the message of Menachem Begin, both in his own voice and as told by others.

Begin was born in Brisk, where his father was Secretary of the Jewish Community. At age sixteen Begin heard Ze'ev Jabotinsky (1880–1940) speak. His life would never be the same. He was mesmerized by the message of Jewish nationalism. Begin joined Betar and quickly rose in its ranks.

From Brisk, Begin moved to Warsaw, but he felt the threat of Polish anti-Semitism and neighboring Nazi Germany, so he moved onward to Vilna. There his political activities soon were interrupted. After the Russian takeover, he was arrested for anti-Soviet activity and sentenced to eight years hard labor in Siberia. Zionism was a crime against the state. After eight months a deal was reached to release Polish citizens including Begin. In August 1942 he made his way to Palestine. His parents remained in Poland, where they met death at the hands of the Nazis.

Begin worked against the British, who labeled him a terrorist. After the State of Israel was declared, he turned politician and served twenty-nine years in the Knesset. His message, though, was not only Greater Israel as advocated by Betar. He stood for a social program benefiting the poor and measures to fully integrate Sephardim into all aspects of Israeli society.

Perhaps Begin will be best remembered for signing the peace treaty with Egypt. There were hard decisions and strong opposition in the negotiation process, but Begin rose above entrenched philosophic ideas and looked to the future. The champion of Greater Israel approved the evacuation of Jewish settlements from the Sinai in favor of the promise of peace.

For most people the main attraction of the Center is the tour. There is also a library based on Begin's personal collection and an archive, each maintained on a separate floor. Use of these facilities is best done by prior arrangement. For the archives a symbolic fee is charged.

The Center is at Rechov Nachon 6, near the Chan Theater. Hours are Sunday–Monday and Wednesday–Thursday, 0900–1630; Tuesday, 0900–1900; Friday, 0900–1200. Closed Shabbat. Tours are NIS 25 for adults; NIS 20 for seniors and children under 18. Tel. 02-565 2020.

Belz Torah Center *(See color plate 20, p. 103)*

The Belz Torah Center is the largest synagogue in the world, where the main sanctuary seats 5,500 people. Yet it is not big enough; for Rosh Hashanah windows are removed on one side of the synagogue, and 300 additional seats are added in a temporary facility outside.

The synagogue is relatively new. Ceremonial groundbreaking took place in 1984 on a desolate hill called Har Komona, and actual construction commenced two years later. Only in 2000 did the building formally open. The two day celebration is symbolic of the Belz philosophy. The first day was devoted to studying Torah; only after people had learned in the building did the dedication take place.

The origin of the Belz Chassidic movement goes back to the small town in the Ukraine from which the movement takes its name. In the early 1800s the first Belzer *Rebbe*, Rabbi Shalom Rokeach (1779–1855), spent 1000 consecutive nights awake learning Torah. On the last night there was a terrible storm, but the *Rebbe* withstood the challenge of the cold and darkness. He continued to learn. Finally, the storm abated, and he was rewarded. *Eliyahu HaNavi* appeared, and taught him the secrets and laws of building a synagogue.

It is a basic tenet of Belz *chassidut* that learning is not enough. One must transform learning into deeds. So, in 1828 Rabbi Rokeach took upon himself to build a synagogue in Belz. He was present in all phases of construction to oversee the minutest detail. The building was finally finished in 1843. Why did construction take fifteen years? It didn't. The men's section was finished long before. The *Rebbe* would not permit use until the women's section was completed. After all, it is the crying and faith of women that help push prayers into Heaven.

The years went by, but history changed on *Shemini Atseret* 1939 as Nazi troops occupied Belz. At age sixty the fourth *Rebbe* miraculously escaped and found successive hiding places until he made his way to the Land of Israel in 1944. Meanwhile, the Germans tried to destroy the synagogue. They tried to knock it down, but they failed. They attempted to blow up the building with dynamite, but again they did not succeed. Only in the 1950s did the Communists take apart the synagogue, literally stone by stone.

Most Belz *Chassidim* did not escape the ruthless Nazi rule in Europe. The *Rebbe* and his brother lost almost their entire families. Today, the past has not been totally wiped out in the town of Belz. The gravestones of the first three *Rebbes* still remain. The future of the movement, however, lay elsewhere—in Jerusalem.

For many years after World War II the headquarters of the Belz movement was in a building on Rechov Agrippas near the Ministry of Foreign Affairs, but the dream of the old synagogue in Europe was not lost. The decision was made to build on Har Komona.

Again, the Belzer *Rebbe* personally oversaw construction. It was to be a building of holiness. Two men selected by the *Rebbe* poured all of the cement saying, "For the holiness of a synagogue," time and time again.

The synagogue that was built stands thirteen stories high (eleven floors are used and the remaining two floors are to give height to the synagogue). The main sanctuary has six entrances, two men's galleries, and four women's galleries. Despite the large size, the acoustics are perfect, as a result of slanted walls and specially designed chandeliers which project sound without an echo. Just do not look for a wall clock to see what time it is—there are no clocks. It is a Belz tradition.

Every aspect of religious life has been carefully considered. The place before the Reader's stand is recessed, to remember, "From the depths I called you." The area where one washes is made of stone, so that it should not be impure. There is even a well outside for *Tashlich* on Rosh Hashanah.

Despite the size of the building, it is functional and not ostentatious. On the fourth floor alone there are seven rabbinic colleges and the largest Torah open-shelf library in Israel. Nor do you have to be a Belzer *Chassid* to use it. Any Jew is more than welcome to sit in one of the three hundred seats in the main *Beit HaMidrash* and learn (open twenty-four hours, of course). Or, one can pray in one of the dozen smaller synagogues in the building.

The Belz Torah Center is open twenty-four hours a day for those who want to pray or study. Busses No. 3, 10. The main synagogue is used on Shabbat and holidays. Tours by prior arrangement.

Bezalel Academy of Art and Design

The Bezalel Academy of Art and Design was the dream of Boris Schatz (1866–1932) of Lithuania, who proposed the founding of the school to Theodor Herzl in 1903. Two years later, at the Seventh Zionist Congress in Basle, a proposal to establish a Jewish school of art was accepted. In 1906 Schatz left his position as Official Court Sculptor in Bulgaria for Palestine and opened the school on Rechov Ethiopia in Jerusalem. In 1908 the school was given two buildings bought from Effendi Abu Shakir on Rechov Shmuel HaNagid. The theme of the academy was Jewish art, so the institution was appropriately named after the Biblical artisan, Bezalel ben Uri ben Hur.

Jewish art was defined in its broadest sense. In 1911 the Academy opened a branch in Ben Shemen to encourage the work of Yemenite silversmiths. World War I, however, forced the closing of that branch and a general stoppage in the productivity of the Bezalel Academy. In 1917 the Ottomans, fearful of Schatz' cultural influence, banished him from Jerusalem to Damascus, then to Tsefat and Tiberias. Schatz, though, returned to Jerusalem after the triumph of British forces. The future of the Academy was uncertain. Finances were difficult, and several times the Academy opened, closed, and then re-opened. Schatz, himself, passed away in 1932 during a fundraising trip. In 1935 the Academy opened again, and it has been in continuous operation ever since. Finally, in 1990 many of the school's operations were transferred to Hebrew University on Mt. Scopus.

The main attractions at Bezalel are periodic art exhibitions which they sponsor. Dates and locations can be ascertained by calling the Academy. There usually is a mixture of both secular and religious art themes.

The Academy on Mount Scopus can be reached at Tel. 02-589 3333. The specialized library is on the ninth floor of the Weiler Building, Tel. 02-589 3277.

Bible Lands Museum *(See color plate 21, p. 104)*

The museum was founded by Dr. Elie Borowski (1913–2003) to bring better understanding to the history and cultures of the nations who interfaced with Biblical and Talmudic events.

Borowski had a clear concept of the museum's mission. He was an observant Jew who learned in Mir Yeshiva before World War II. Borowski's family would not leave Poland while they still could, but Borowski did leave, enlisted in a special unit in the French army, and fought against the Nazis before retreat to Switzerland. It was there that Borowski found an ancient seal mentioning a Biblical monarch. That was the beginning of what would be a collection of some 2500 seals. It is not surprising that an important segment of the museum is dedicated to seals and their development. Of special interest are seals from Judea, dating to 711–705 BCE.

In Egypt the rings of Pharaoh and the aristocratic class included a seal (see Genesis 41:42 and Nachmanides on the verse). Examples on display are cylindrical seals. Displays also show the development of writing on seals from cuneiform to hieroglyphics to hieratic script.

Even in ancient times people cherished their privacy. Many inscriptions are meant for public documents, but at times someone wants to write a private letter to be read only by the intended recipient. Today we routinely do this by placing a letter in a closed envelope. The same was done in ancient times; one exhibit shows "envelopes" of clay with tablets inserted inside.

The Sumerian Room gives good insight into the world that Abraham ridiculed in Ur. There is a reconstruction of the local *Ziggurat*, a temple of idol worship built on high ground to show the connection between heaven and earth. There is also a collection of idols—portable ones to take along for protection, and stationary ones to guard one's house. Not to be forgotten, there are even idols that pray for the owner in front of yet other idols.

Ancient Egypt was a center of idol worship and paganism. There is an authentic illustration showing ritual slaughter and subsequent drinking of blood. A painted coffin depicts two eyes—the indication at which end of the coffin the deceased's head was placed. There is a mummy case in the museum, but in deference to *cohanim*, there is no corpse inside; there are also empty canopic jars (1550–1307 BCE), once used to store body organs upon mummification.

Considerable effort was made to bring a better understanding to Shushan. The new capital was inaugurated by Darius, the father of Achashverosh. A model of the *apadana* (reception hall) in the royal palace (based on the Bible and archeological findings) shows that it was an extremely tall edifice of monumental proportions, inspiring awe and fear amongst the citizens of Shushan.

The treatment given to the palace of Sennacherib in Nineveh is similar. There is a model of the palace as well as a limestone relief of Sennacherib fighting in Lebanon.

This is only a sampling of what is to be seen in the museum. A catalogue contains extensive pictures of the exhibits, but it is not a substitute for a properly guided tour.

The museum is at Rechov Granot 25 (Museum Row) and is open Sunday, Monday, Tuesday and Thursday 0930–1730; Wednesday 0930–2130; and Friday 0930–1400. Closed Shabbat. Entrance fee: NIS 32 for adults, NIS 20 for children, and NIS 16 for senior citizens. Tel. 02-561 1066.

Buses 9, 17, 24, 99. One hour guided tours in English are conducted daily at 1015 and on Wednesdays again at 1730. A typical visit takes between two and three hours.

Biblical Zoo

Fact: An unexpectedly large number of adults visit Jerusalem's Biblical Zoo, many unaccompanied by children. The reality is that the zoo is for everyone.

The easiest way to see the sixty-two acre zoo is to take the "train" (adults NIS 2, children NIS 1) to Noah's Ark, then walk the two kilometer (1.25 mile) path back to the entrance/exit gates.

Biblical Zoo.
[Giraffe, Oryx, and Sheepl] (Sheina)

Noah's Ark, an exhibit Center with souvenir shop and refreshments stand, symbolizes and important role that the zoo has taken upon itself. The Biblical Zoo is not only a collection of animals, many known from Biblical verses, but also an important institution in the effort to save animal species from extinction, particularly in Israel.

The oryx, for example, is virtually extinct. This is just one example of the zoo's efforts to save animals from extinction.

Another example is the fallow deer mentioned in Deuteronomy 14:5, which has been extinct in Eretz Yisrael since the nineteenth century, due in major part to uncontrolled hunting. In the 1950s it was learnt that some of these deer existed in Iran. Negotiations to bring the deer to Israel were protracted. Finally, one male and four female fallow deer were sent on the last flight from Teheran to Tel Aviv before the fall of the Shah! They were brought to Haifa for breeding. Today, the third generation of "sabra" fallow deer are kept at the zoo. Others are left wild but under supervision in the Galilee near Maalot.

Another animal mentioned in the same verse and found at the zoo is the addax, which is listed as kosher. Yet, it was never brought as a sacrifice. The reason is brought in rabbinic literature by Rabbi Yehudah Bar Simon. The addax lived in mountainous areas, and it was extremely difficult to catch. We were not given commandments too difficult to fulfill.

Believe it or not, lions (the Asiatic strain) wandered freely in Eretz Yisrael, until they were killed off by hunters. There is a fenced area for lions at the zoo, but do not worry. The lions cannot escape. By the way, do not think of keeping your own pet lion. Keeping one can be very expensive. A lion typically eats twenty-five kg. (fifty-five lb.) of meat at each meal.

Without a question, elephants are the biggest eaters at the zoo. They spend three quarters of their lives eating. That adds up to between 75 kg.

(165 lb.) and 115 kg. (253 lb.) per day. Luckily, though, they are vegetarians. Their basic diet is grass, twigs, and tree bark.

A curiosity. One does not usually associate a hippopotamus with *Eretz Yisrael*. Nor is one mentioned in the Bible. Yet, bones of a hippopotamus dating to the era of the Judges were found in the Yarkon area.

Not everything at the zoo is animals. There is a "tropical rain forest" housing an aviary. Remember that 25 percent of medicines have components that originate in rain forest plants. There are some two thousand plants with a medicinal effect in the treatment of various tumors.

The Biblical Zoo is not new to Jerusalem. It started out during the British Mandate on today's Rechov Rabbi Kook, just off Jaffa Road. In 1941 it moved to Shmuel HaNavi, then to the Hebrew University on Mount Scopus. There, Professor Aharon Synagogueov (1907–1997) of the Zoology Department gave it the name, Biblical Zoo. Synagogueov was born in the Ukraine, where he was imprisoned for Zionist activities. He escaped to Palestine and became a world-renown entomologist.

The Zoo was a casualty of the War of Independence. Some animals ran away during the fighting. Others perished, as food became more and more of a problem. By 1951 the remaining animals had been transported to Jewish Jerusalem in the bi-weekly caravans, so a formal zoo was opened in Romema. That facility, however, grew too small, and land in the area became prohibitively expensive for expansion. The Romema zoo was closed in 1991, and the new Biblical Zoo in Malcha was opened in 1993.

A visit to the Biblical Zoo is definitely recommended, Bible in hand. Animals mentioned in Biblical verses cease to be just "another creature." They take on new meaning, as the visitor sees exactly what they are.

The zoo is open to the public Sunday–Friday from 0900 until 1700 winter), 1800 (spring and fall), or 1900 (summer), and on Shabbat. The zoo does not sell tickets on Shabbat; they must be purchased in advance or from a private vendor. During the summer visits are recommended in late afternoon, when temperatures begin to cool off. Adults NIS 41. Children (three years and older) and senior citizens NIS 33. Tel. 02-675 0111.

The zoo can be reached by the 26 bus, which runs twice an hour during most of the day.

Bloomfield Science Museum *(See color plate 22, p. 104)*

Popular rumor is that Albert Einstein (1879–1955) was a poor student. After all, he received fives and sixes on his report card (except for three in French). Poor student? No! This is a classic example of how our minds work. We have been trained to consider ten as the highest grade. In Einstein's school the highest grade was six.

The Bloomfield Science museum first opened in 1992 then was expanded in 2000. It is the dream of Peter Hillman, Professor of Physics and Neurobiology at Hebrew University. Except for special exhibits, the entire museum is interactive, built with the intent of displaying scientific principles through reading captions, seeing demonstrations, and—most important—engaging in activities. All guides are advanced students of science, primarily at Hebrew University.

The Einstein report card is just one indication of how we have been trained to think. At the entrance to the museum there was an exhibit (subject to change) about how the mind works. Pick up two tubes. We expect the smaller one to be lighter. The mind even transmits this expectation to our feelings. A man and woman wearing formal attire are presented in a picture. We are trained to see two different people, but under close examination it is clear that both are the same. A face is shown upside down. Looking at it one assumes that all is normal, yet turn it right-side up, and it is evident that the man has an exaggerated frown even bordering on anguish.

Children play with toys, and one exhibit shows how some of those toys work. Seven metal balls are hung together in a row. Move the ball at the far left further to the left, release it, and let it strike the next ball; the ball farthest to the right will receive the force and move. Move two balls farther to the left and release them; correct, the two balls to the right will move. But what happens if you move five of the seven balls to the left and release them? The five balls to the right (including three of the five that were pulled left) will move to the right.

Large capsules are loaded with weights, and then placed on a moving surface. Rotate the surface to the right, or to the left. The position of the capsules shows the effects of gravity.

We all turn on lights. How hot is it inside the bulb? One exhibit allows a user to adjust the intensity of the light and see how that affects the temperature inside the bulb. Another exhibit shows what happens when plain air, argon (Ar), and helium (He) are injected into a neon light.

The questions are endless. How do medicines work? What are the active characteristics of pills and capsules? Creams and ointments? Extensive space is allocated to explaining the answers. There is also an explanation about the history of medicine in Israel. Medicines began to be produced in the country during World War I, when supply from abroad was problematic. During the 1920s the British brought order to the situation and issued a codex to control medicines.

How do communications work? Another exhibit shows the three stages: encoding, modulation (transmission), and decoding. The emphasis is on techniques, since "gadgets" change very rapidly.

All signs in the museum are trilingual—Hebrew, English, and Arabic. There is a very special exhibit about mathematics, that has also been displayed at Al-Quds University in the Palestinian Authority. Seeing Arab school children tour the museum is another real indication of coexistence between Jews and Arabs.

Perhaps the bottom line in seeing this museum is arriving at a better appreciation of the world that the Almighty created.

Rechov Rupin. Monday–Thursday 1000–1800. Friday 1000–1400. Closed Sundays. Not Shomer Shabbat. Longer hours during vacations and Chol HaMoed. Fees: Children 0–5 free, 6–18 NIS 25, Adults NIS 30, Family NIS 100. Fees during vacations and holidays: Individuals NIS 35, Family NIS 125. Tel. 02-654 4888. Wheelchair accessible.

Bukharian Neighborhood

The Bukharian area adjoining Geula and Mea Shearim was built by wealthy Jews from Bukhara, Samarkand and Tashkent who constructed virtual mansions for themselves, some of them "summer homes."

These Jews came to Jerusalem in the 1870s and 1880s. They bought the land for their houses and employed Conrad Schick (1822–1901) to plan construction so that, "the arrangement and style of building should follow European practice, that the quarter become a proud part of Jerusalem." The new neighborhood was called "Rechovot," but the name was replaced by a nickname—the Quarter of the Bukharians. In time the nickname became official.

Construction in the neighborhood began in the 1890s, but even from the beginning there were unexpected problems. The Ottoman army requisitioned buildings for its use. After the Russian Revolution of 1917 residents of the neighborhood were cut off from their countries of origin (and in many cases from their sources of income). Soon the neighborhood was no longer the center of wealth that had been envisioned.

Over the years notable people lived in the neighborhood. They were well-known, but not rich: Yitzhak Ben-Zvi (1884–1963) (to become Israel's second President); Moshe Sharett (1894–1965) (later Prime Minister); and Professor Joseph Klausner (1874–1958) of Hebrew University.

Today the neighborhood is within the zone of no Shabbat traffic permitted on the streets. The best known building in the Bukharian Quarter is the Mussayif Synagogue, where one can find a minyan (Sephardic rite) at virtually every hour from early morning through very late evening. The synagogue was started by Shlomo Mussayif, who was born in Bukhara in 1851 and immigrated to Israel in 1890. In 1894 he built his house and the synagogue that still bears his name. Shlomo Mussayif died in 1921 and is interred on the Mount of Olives.

Chagall Windows

In 1962 the French Jewish artist, Marc Chagall (1909–1992), donated twelve stained glass windows depicting the Twelve Tribes to Hadassah-Ein Karem Hospital. These are part of the Abbell Synagogue at the hospital.

The windows can be seen Sunday–Thursday 0800–1315 and 1400–1530. Tel. 02-677 6271. Busses 19, 27, 42.

Davidka

The Davidka, a legendary weapon of the War for Independence, sits on a pedestal opposite the Clal Building at R. Jaffa 97. People think that the Davidka was of little or no offensive value making noises loud enough to scare off the enemy. The Davidka was a relatively primitive Israeli mortar that made thundering noise. But the Davidka was not a useless weapon. It is naïve to believe that the Arab Legion and its supporters could be scared off so easily—perhaps the first or second times, but not thereafter. The Davidka fired sixty pounds of TNT in a ninety-pound shell, which was quite lethal in a direct hit. It also spread significant amounts of shrapnel. The basic problem was that the Davidka was quite inaccurate.

The etymology of "Davidka" is not "Little David," recalling the story of David confronting the giant Goliath. The Davidka is named after its designer, David Leibowitch, while he was working at the Mikveh Israel agricultural school in Holon during the winter, 1947–1948. In all, Leibowitch made six of these weapons.

The Davidka first saw its use in combat on 13 March 1948, as Jewish forces attacked the Abu Kabir neighborhood of Jaffa. The Davidka on display in Jerusalem is in what has become known as Davidka Square. The weapon was part of deployment for defense of Jerusalem.

Geula

Bikur Holim Hospital

The hospital dates back to a very unsuitable residential building in the Old City in 1826 and the *aliya* several years earlier of the students of the

Vilna Gaon. The handful of Jewish residents had begun to grow, and there had to be some kind of organized medical care. The 1826 hospital struggled along. By 1843 Bikur Holim consisted of three rooms for patients—not exactly enough to serve even a very small community.

The *yishuv* was hard-pressed for funds. Sir Moses Montefiore deserves special mention. He donated large quantities of medicines for use by those being treated.

In 1854 a building was purchased for Bikur Holim, but within ten years it, too, became obsolete. It was insufficient, as Jews began to filter into Jerusalem, and the city started to expand outside the walls. The next solution came in 1864, when a courtyard with two not very large buildings was purchased; the buildings were for medical treatment, a pharmacy, a hospice for the terminally ill, and administrative offices. The opening of the "new and enlarged" hospital came none too soon. In 1866 the facility treated numerous patients after an outbreak of cholera in Jerusalem.

Bikur Holim, "the Ashkenazi Perushim Hospital," was a favorite charity of Montefiore. In his diary he described the facility as it was in 1875. The general ward consisted of two rooms, each with eight beds. One room was reserved for men, and the other was restricted to women.

The hospital went from one financial crisis to another, but medicine never stopped. Administration was streamlined, but the sick continued to be treated. In 1893, for example, 781 patients were hospitalized, and 12,347 people were treated as outpatients.

Jerusalem was becoming a different city than it had been. The Jewish population was increasing, and new neighborhoods took root outside the city walls. Medicine was changing. The old Bikur Holim could no longer serve the city as it had in the past. Soon hospitalizations exceeded one thousand *per annum*.

In 1898 Kaiser Wilhelm II (1859–1941) visited Jerusalem and made a triumphal entry into the city as multitudes gathered to welcome him. The Kaiser left his mark on Jerusalem. Amongst other things he donated a large sum of money which was used by Bikur Holim Hospital to purchase the grounds where the current medical center stands on Rechov Straus.

Despite Wilhelm's support of the hospital he periodically was quoted in rabid anti-Semitic outbursts, for example calling Jews "parasites" holding "nefarious positions." Some say the motivation was a deep-seated hate of Jews; others contend that the Kaiser recklessly and irrationally searched for a scapegoat as he became increasingly embittered by his personal misfortunes and difficulties.

The Kaiser's six-day visit to Jerusalem was royal in every sense. "Tent City" was erected on today's Rechov Ha-Nevi'im (Prophets Street), near

Bikur Holim. The tents were not standard army issue. Four grandiose parlor tents were specially sent by the Ottoman Sultan, who sought to align himself politically with Germany. There were also six kitchen tents to prepare food for the two hundred person entourage.

Wilhelm II left an indelible stamp on Jerusalem. He dedicated buildings, and streets were paved in his honor. History, however, has not treated him kindly. There are those who contend that his political machinations were inept and a major cause of World War I. Others argue that the Kaiser had every intention of going to war, and merely waited for what he considered the most appropriate opportunity. In any event, his army lost the war, and he was forced to abdicate.

After the Great War Wilhelm II fled Germany and took refuge in the Netherlands, where he was granted asylum from calls that he be tried for war crimes by an international tribunal.

The Kaiser demonstrated staunch opposition to the Nazi Party, not for any concern for Jews, but as indicative of his dedication to Germany— in his delusions to be again ruled by his family, of course. (At one point he promoted one of his grandchildren for ascendancy to the throne, but the move gained no real public support.) When one son later expressed Nazi sympathies, he was quietly declared an outcast by the family.

In 1907 a decision at Bikur Holim was taken. A hospital would be built in New Jerusalem. Residents of the Old City were afraid of the change, but endorsement of the move by key rabbis of the time—Berlin, Salant, Sonnenfeld, Kook—muted opposition.

The cornerstone of the new building was laid in 1912, but with the outbreak of the "Great War" two years later, construction was halted until after Ottoman surrender in Jerusalem and the general Armistice in 1918. The pressure to build, however, was unabated. By 1913 there were more than 65,000 outpatients treated by Bikur Holim, five times as many as twenty years previously.

Times were changing. The Ottoman Empire had fallen. The British took over. There were Arab riots. Construction on the new Bikur Holim building was slow, but by 1925 it was finished. Bikur Holim, a modern hospital for all of the city's residents—Jews and non-Jews alike —opened on King George V Street[3] just off Jaffa Road. (The hospital in the Old City was not closed. It was used to treat the chronically ill until 1947, when British troops helped transfer the besieged sick to the Rechov Straus facility.)

The history of the hospital during the next two decades was, in many ways, a microcosm of life during the Mandate. Many of the wounded from

---

[3] Currently Rechov King George is only that segment of the street on the other side of Jaffa Road.

the Arab riots of 1929 and 1936 were brought to Bikur Holim. Wounded Jewish underground fighters were hospitalized with ruses in record keeping, so that the Mandate police could not discover their true identities and affiliation.

During the fighting of 1948 the hospital came under artillery fire from Arab guns. The halls of the hospital were crowded with the wounded. Hadassah Hospital was evacuated from Mount Scopus, and many of the patients were transferred to Bikur Holim. But, the hospital was entering a new stage of its history. It was a major medical facility just off the downtown area of the new Israeli capital.

There is no historical exhibit to see in Bikur Holim. The buildings, though, are architectural gems of their period. The story of the hospital is interesting and should not be forgotten.

Today one very unique specialty of the hospital is the treatment of male fertility problems, of course according to Jewish Law.

Geula Neighborhood

In relatively recent years Geula has become a major center for ultra-orthodox Jewry in Jerusalem, as it received a population spill-over from adjacent Mea Shearim. Geula is also a popular shopping area for religious goods and clothing appropriate for laws of modesty. The main street is Rechov Malchei Yisrael.

Geula originally began as two separate neighborhoods:

(1) *Kerem Avraham* (Abraham's Vineyard), on the side of Rechov Malchei Yisrael farther from the center of Jerusalem, was bought in 1852 by the wife of the British Consul, James Fine. She envisioned a missionary effort to employ Jews and draw them to Christianity. Her efforts failed, and the land was sold to Jews. In 1930 *Kerem Avraham* was joined officially with Geula; residential building commenced in the neighborhood with Rechov Yechezkael (paved in 1937) then as the main street.

(2) In 1861 Johann Ludwig Schneller (1820–1896), a German missionary, built the German "Schneller Orphanage" along what is now Rechov Malchei Yisrael on land he had purchased from Arab villagers of Lifta in 1856. The orphanage complex consisted of eight buildings constructed in a mixture of German and Middle Eastern styles.

The orphanage started modestly in a two room building, but soon it grew to be the largest orphanage in Jerusalem. At one time it housed 180 mostly Arab orphans.

Schneller's motive was not altruistic concern for the unfortunate and needy. His major purpose was to convert people to Christianity. In 1891 he admitted failure; the orphans whom he housed returned to their villages and returned to Islam. In May 1894 the orphanage officially became a center for evangelicalism, promoting the Lutheran faith.

At the beginning of World War II the Germans were expelled from Schneller, and the Lutheran center was closed. The buildings became a British army base. In 1948 "Schneller" was taken by Jewish forces and served first as a Haganah facility, then an Israeli Army base, providing a quick military response to the nearby Jordanian border in divided Jerusalem. Today some of the area has been redeveloped. The rest of the former orphanage was evacuated by the IDF at the end of 2008.

The Lutheran orphanage also owned numerous plots of land in the area between Schneller and Mea Shearim. The land was rocky and unsuitable for agricultural cultivation. So, the "Schneller Woods" was sold to the Schloush brothers of Jaffa for residential development.

Avraham, Chaim and Yosef Schloush were businessmen. They divided the land in the "Schloush Neighborhood," and sold off the plots. Business and money were foremost, and there was no room for charity. When neighborhood leader Ze'ev Spiegel suggested that the brothers build a synagogue, the proposition was met with a flat refusal. In his pique Spiegel suggested that the name of the neighborhood be changed from the "Schloush Neighborhood," to Geula ("redeemed" from the Christians). Schloush is now little more than a footnote in history books.

Rechov Straus

A main street in Geula is Rechov Straus, leading from Jaffa Road to Kikar Shabbat. *(See color plate 23, p. 104)* Called Chancellor Avenue in Mandate times (a ceramic sign can still be seen at Kikar Shabbat), the name was changed to Rechov Straus in memory of Nathan Straus (1848–1931), an American philanthropist and New York City Parks commissioner (1889–1893).

In 1912 two brothers, Nathan and Isidor Straus (born 1845), the owners of R.H. Macy's Department Store and founders of the A&S (Abraham & Straus) chain, were touring Europe. In an impulsive decision, they choose to visit Palestine.

After viewing the poverty of Palestine, Nathan remained and looked to develop programs to help Jews. Isidor Straus returned to Europe and set sail for New York on the luxury ocean liner on which his brother also had held booking.

Nathan finally left Palestine and hurried to England, only to find that the ship had already left Southampton port. That ship was the Titanic. Isidor and his wife, Ida, did not survive.

Guela. Mandate street sign in Kikar Shabbat

Nathan was shaken by the experience and increased his philanthropic work as a gesture of gratitude. When the State of Israel was declared, the city of Netanya, which he had helped establish, and Rechov Straus were named after him.

Today Rechov Straus is a popular shopping street. It is also home to the headquarters of the *Eida Chareidit*. When Hadassah Hospital was moved from Mt. Scopus in 1948, it occupied several buildings on Rechov Straus (also spelled Strauss).

Rechov Yishayahu runs parallel to Rechov Straus. On the corner of Yishayahu and Yitzchak Prag (connecting to Straus) there is an incongruous building for a Jewish neighborhood—an Islamic Mosque. Moslems never lived in the area. From its inception as a residential area, only Jews lived there. The building, Qubba al-Qatmuriyya (a mausoleum and prayer area belonging to a Kurdish family), was built no later than 1251 and contains the graves of four martyrs who met their deaths in battle at that time and another who was killed in 1368.

Givat Shaul (Biblical) *(See color plate 24, p. 104)*

The verse in I Samuel 15:34 is clear, "Shaul went up to his home [presumably a palace, per Radaq (1160–1235)] at Givat Shaul." The unanswered question is, "Where was Givat Shaul located?"

The palace of Shaul the King was definitely not located near today's Givat Shaul at the western entrance to Jerusalem. The name is fitting, but not the history. Today's Givat Shaul was developed starting in the early twentieth century, and major construction projects continued into the 1960s. The neighborhood is named after Rabbi Yaakov Shaul Elishar (1817–1909), author of *Yisa' B'racha* and various other religious texts. The land was purchased from the Arab villages of Deir Yassin and Lifta by Rabbi Nissim Elishar, Arieh Leib and Moshe Kopel Kantrovitz. The first settlers were mostly Yemenite Jewish farmers.

Rabbi Elishar was born in Tsfat. Six years later his family moved to Jerusalem, where he studied, then commenced a rabbinic career that would eventually lead to the position of Chief Sephardic Rabbi of Ottoman Palestine. He was also in routine correspondence with Rabbi Yosef Chaim ben Elija (1834–1909), better known as the Ben Ish Hai. Rabbi Elishar passed away in 1906, and one of his sons was instrumental in having the new neighborhood named after him.

Biblical Givat Shaul is on a quiet hilltop today known as Tel al-Ful, some two hundred meters (650 feet) to the east of Nablus Road at the southern end of the modern Beit Hanina neighborhood and just outside Pisgat Ze'ev. Tel Al-Ful is about an hour's walk from the mountain that was destined to be the Temple Mount.

Tel al-Ful is not well developed. It is a relatively barren area with a dirt path winding up the hilltop from a local school. Several houses dot the slopes, but the population is sparse. Yet, the climb is definitely worthwhile. Once atop the hill there is a breath-taking view of Jerusalem, seen in 360 degree panorama without visual obstruction. According to Biblical commentators there is a question whether the hilltop was pre-existent, or if Shaul built it. In either case, the lookout over the topography is also militarily strategic.

Shaul was not the only monarch interested in Tel a-Ful. In 1963 King Hussein (1935–1999) of Jordan, then ruling over the West Bank and East Jerusalem, razed houses on the site and started building a palace. He had used rented properties in Beit Hanina when he came to Jerusalem, but he wanted something more permanent. Construction, however, was abruptly halted in 1967, during the Six Day War. Jordan lost control of the area, and the concrete shell of the royal palace was abandoned.

Today, Tel al-Ful awaits the archeologist's shovel, but there are no immediate plans to dig on the site. The issue is politically sensitive, since the hilltop still belongs to the royal Hashemite family in Amman, although it is administered by the Israeli office for abandoned properties.

Some excavations cannot be planned. Recently, the Orine Jewish settlement just under Givat Sha'ul on the Jerusalem-Ramallah road was discovered accidentally. In digging to install the light rail network to Neve-Yaakov, construction workers stumbled upon a considerable part of this first–second century settlement. The current hypothesis is that after the Destruction of the Second Temple, Jews were allowed to settle close to Roman-ruled Jerusalem, so they settled in Orine. After the Bar Kochba Revolt and the establishment of Aelia Capitolina, Orine was destroyed. There was no place for Jews near Jerusalem. The Romans made every effort to keep Jews out of Judea.

To reach Tel al-Ful it is best to go by car, since connections by bus are poor. Drive north on Nablus Road past Shuafat. Turn right at the first sign to Pisgat Ze'ev, then make the first left, and drive until the end of the road. Park and walk up the path. It is recommended not to make a visit without a companion.

Great Synagogue *(See color plate 25, p. 105)*

On Tu B'Av 5742 (4 August 1982) the Great Synagogue opened at Rechov King George 56, adjacent to Heichal Shlomo on land purchased with the initiative of Dr. Maurice Jaffe. The entirely private project was envisioned as a monument to the State of Israel. It was constructed in memory of Holocaust victims and those fallen while defending the Jewish State. The Great Synagogue has no official status, nor does it receive any government funding.

The name of the synagogue is quite bombastic and presumptuous, but there is no denying that this Jerusalem synagogue is certainly impressive. Designed by Alexander Friedman and built with the financial support of Sir Isaac (1897–1991) and Lady Wolffson, the synagogue takes into consideration all religious customs. An opening in the roof accommodates a *chupah*. Chairs are adjustable, so they can be lowered for Tisha B'Av. Shelves are designed to facilitate a prayerbook, while the person praying is standing or sitting. There is a place to store a hat, and even a holder for an *etrog*.

The main sanctuary seats 850 men and 550 women in a semi-circular pattern reminiscent of Sephardic synagogues, so that an intimacy is maintained with no more than eleven rows in any direction. Yet, there is a very formal atmosphere that permeates the sanctuary. Perhaps it is because of the chairs reserved for the President of Israel and the Prime Minister, or the seats saved for the Chief Rabbis. The front stained glass window designed by Régine Heim of Zürich draws attention, but the complicated motifs add to a "heavy" atmosphere.

The late-Rabbi Zalman Druck (1934-2009), an Orthodox rabbi, was the *Rov* of the synagogue from its founding until his death in December

2009. A visit to the synagogue is recommended, particularly for aficionados of cantor and choir. (On weekdays there are Ashkenazi and Sephardic *minyanim* in smaller rooms, and daily religious classes offered in Hebrew from 0900-1300–open to the public at no fee.)

The Rosenbaum Mezuzah Collection on display in the entrance hallway is absolutely unrivaled elsewhere. Many of the several hundred mezuzah cases are merely artistic expressions, but some are worthy of special mention.

One special mezuzah case has the letters *shin, daled, yod* written in Braille.

The Rosenbaum's visited one store as they built their collection, and they were puzzled to see that all of the cases offered for sale were in an identical and very unusual shape. They queried the store owner who offered an explanation. When he was an inmate in a concentration camp, he kept a mezuzah parchment with him, but he had no case for it. So, he took a crumbled piece of paper torn from a brown bag, wrapped it around the parchment, and folded the top and bottom closed. He was convinced that keeping this mezuzah saved his life. After his liberation and arrival in Israel in 1950, every mezuzah case that he has made is in the shape and color of the crumbled paper.

Another very different mezuzah case is cherished particularly by Breslov *Chassidim*. In 1808 the Rebbe was presented with a special chair with intricate carvings. After the passing of Rabbi Nachman (1772–1810), the chair was hidden to save it from destruction. In 1936 it was smuggled to Palestine, piece by piece. It was, however, in extremely bad condition. Finally, in 1985 Catriel Sugarman, a renowned Jerusalem artist, was commissioned to restore the chair. He made a mezuzah case from wood pieces that could not be incorporated into the chair.

A final example of an unusual mezuzah case on display is a slice of a tree with artwork on it depicting a biblical scene with Rivka. This hardly looks like a mezuzah case! That was the entire point. This is an artifact designed by a Morrano descendant from Belmonte, Portugal. It is a reminder of the struggle of his ancestors to keep *mitzvot* in an atmosphere where the penalty was death.

Rechov King George 56. The Great Synagogue and the Rosenbaum Mezuzah Collection are open Sunday–Thursday, 0900–1300. Entrance is *gratis*. The main synagogue can also been seen during Shabbat and holiday services (except Rosh Hashana and Yom Kippur. It is best to call ahead to verify unannounced weekday closing. Tel. 02-623 0628 or 052-389 5190. Tours are available with prior notice for groups only. There is a handicapped entrance to the men's section, but not to the women's.

Note: The Yeshurun Synagogue is a block away in the direction of Jaffa Road. It was built in 1934–1936 as the first modern Orthodox synagogue in Jerusalem. It was designed in *bauhaus* style by Meir Rubin and Alexander Friedman.

Gush Katif Museum *(See color plate 26, p. 105)*

Current realities often distort our understanding of past history. Arab control of Gaza, for example, has left the impression that the area is outside the Land of Israel and has no inherent Jewish history. This impression is reinforced by the story of Samson that takes place in Philistine-controlled Gaza. The Gush Katif Museum, on a side street next to Jerusalem's old Shaarei Zedek Hospital, shows very convincingly that Jews did live in Gaza. The area was conquered by the invading Israelites (Judges 1:18). During the Hasmonean period Jews once again conquered Gaza and settled there, only to be exiled in 61 BCE. That exile, however, was not permanent. Some two hundred years later Jews returned.

A remnant of Jews in Gaza is a mosaic made in 508–509 CE and recovered from the ruins of an 800 square meter (8,600 square feet) synagogue situated near the port. The mosaic, now in storage at the Rockefeller Museum, serves as tangible proof of a Jewish presence in the city, which apparently continued until the medieval Arab conquest.

Jews again lived in the city from the Mamluk period until the attempted Napoleonic conquest of Palestine in 1799. Settlement was renewed in 1885, and a school was started in 1910. In 1929, however, Jewish presence in Gaza came to an end, as Jews fled Arab riots and sought shelter in a British hotel. They were evacuated to Tel Aviv in the middle of the night. A new kibbutz began in Kfar Darom in 1946, but it was abandoned on 8 July 1948 after staunch but futile resistance to the advancing Egyptian army.

11 October 1970 ushered in a new chapter in the history of Jewish presence with the coming of a Nachal group to Kfar Darom. Then more Jews came. By 2004 there were twenty settlements (seventeen religious) with five schools and six yeshivot, a seminary for girls, agriculture and industry.

The museum depicts life during the heyday of the Gush and documents the sad events in the week beginning on 17 August 2005. After an essentially non-negotiable Israeli government decision, Jewish Gaza was evacuated. IDF soldiers and Israel Police dismantled more than twenty-five years of building. Many of the uniformed Israelis were in tears as they complied with orders from commanders. Was the evacuation justified? The

Gush Katif Museum provides pictures and statistics to help the visitor decide for himself.

There are serious *halachic* questions regarding the Israeli uprooting of Jewish settlement in what is Eretz Yisrael. This museum rightfully makes no effort to resolve those issues. In the tour only one very clear rabbinic decision is highlighted. The Israeli government honoured the directive of Rabbi Eliashiv; synagogues and yeshivot were emptied of their contents, but the buildings remained intact until the Arabs wrought upon them wanton destruction. Bodies were also exhumed from cemeteries and re-buried in Israel. Rather than *halachic* discourse, however, the museum focuses on the graphic description of the emotional toll of removing people from their homes and from their land.

As a Jewish area Gush Katif flourished. Now government buildings have been taken over by the Palestinian Authority, but fields lay fallow, yeshivas are in ruins, and looted houses are deteriorating.

Note: Most exhibits, but not all, do contain both Hebrew and English explanations. In any event a guided tour (available in Hebrew with advance notice) is much more effective than an unescorted visit.

The museum is at Rechov Shaarei Zedek 5, Jerusalem. Open Sunday–Thursdays 1100–1600, Friday 0900–1300. Expanded hours during Chol HaMoed. Closed Shabbat and holidays. Tel. 02-625 5456. Entrance fee: NIS 10. Not wheelchair accessible.

Har Mamenuchot and other Cemeteries

Har Hamenuchot was opened during the fall 1951 as the general Jewish cemetery for Jerusalem. There are numerous Torah personalities who are buried there, including: Chaim Joseph David Azulai ("Chida") (1724–1807, reburied) *(See color plate 28, p. 106)*, Eliyahu Chaim Carlebach (1925–1990) (Encyclopedia of Chasidus), Moshe Feinstein (1895–1986) (Igrot Moshe), Yitzchak Kadouri (died 2006) (mystic), Aharon Kotler (1891–1962) (Lakewood Yeshiva), Isser Zalman Meltzer (1870–1953) (Even HaEzel), Aharon Rokeach (1877–1957) (Fourth Belzer Rebbe), Gedalia Schorr (1910–1979) (Ohr Gedaliah), HaRav Shlomo Zalman Auerbach (1910-1995) *(See color pate 27, p. 106)*, and Meir Shapiro (1887–1933, reburied in Jerusalem 1958) (Rosh Yeshivah, Chachmei Lublin). The grave of the second President of Israel, Yitzchak Ben-Zvi (1884–1963), is also on Har Hamenuchot.

There are both Ashkenazi and Sephardic eulogy halls outside the cemetery, as well as bathrooms and sinks for washing.

The cemetery is extremely large, and there is no internal public transportation.

Hebrew University at Givat Ram

Botanical Gardens

In 1954, after the Hebrew University was relocated to Givat Ram a botanical garden was started near the library. In 1962 a new area was designated for the botanical garden, and North American conifers were planted. The garden eventually became a joint project of the university, the Jewish municipality and the Jewish National Fund. Shlomo Aronson, an architect, designed the layout of the garden, which was formally opened in 1985.

Today the Botanical Gardens, managed by the Botanical Garden Association, contain more than 6000 species of plants grown in an area about 120,000 square meters (29.65 acres).

Open Sunday–Thursday 0800–sunset, Friday 0800–1500. Guided tours by prior arrangement. Entrance is from Rechov Yehudah Burla; exit is in Givat Ram. A fee is charged. Tel. 02-679 4012.

National and University Library

The name is misleading. The Israel National and University Library is more than a repository of Israeli publications or a place for college students to prepare term papers. Today the library is the largest repository of Judaica in the world—truly, a library of the Jewish people.

The library began modestly in 1892, when the newly founded B'nai B'rith lodge in Jerusalem decided to house a collection of books in its offices on Ethiopia Street. Some 16,000 volumes were donated by Dr. Moshe Chazanovitch, who shipped them from his home in Bialystok after a trip he made to Jerusalem. Ultra-orthodox Jews in nearby Mea Shearim objected strenuously, and a ban was declared in fear that Jews would be misled by improper books. Slowly, the attitude changed. In 1925 the library became associated with Hebrew University, founded in that year, and a Breslov chassid was given a key position in running the Judaica collection. On 15 April 1930 a new university library incorporating the national library was opened on Mt. Scopus in the David Wolffson Building.

Even during the Mandate the library's national status was unchallenged. A law, continued after the State of Israel was declared, required that two copies of every publication be deposited in the library. One copy is archived; the other is made available for public use.

Crisis came in 1948 when Mt. Scopus was isolated from the Jewish part of the city, and access was restricted. Over a period of almost six years the book collection was transferred to various locations in West Jerusalem by bi-weekly escorted trips of Israeli police who guarded the Mt. Scopus enclave. The current building in Givat Ram was opened in 1960. A large stained glass window designed by Mordechai Ardon and illustrating Isaiah's dream of peace dominates the storey with the main reading rooms.

The material in the library is outstanding. The oldest manuscript held is *Keter Damesk*, a tenth century Pentateuch. There is also a Bible from 1260 and a manuscript containing two tractates of Mishna (*Moed*, *Nashim*) with commentary in the handwriting of the Rambam. Clearly, rare manuscripts are difficult to obtain. In 1949 David Ben Gurion made a key decision. He supported the idea that when original manuscripts cannot be obtained, the library should procure microfilm copies, so that it would hold as much important Judaica as possible. That resolve formed the basis of today's Institute of Microfilmed Manuscripts, which holds some 74,000 reels containing 95 percent of known Hebrew manuscripts.

The library owns about two-thirds of the incunabula (the 140 or so Hebrew books printed in the years 1450–1500), including a 1480 full printing of the Rambam's *Mishna Torah*. You cannot walk in and look at these rare items, since they are kept under strict environmental controls. Facsimiles, however, of most materials are available. The library is also keeping up with modern technology; they have started a digital repository of incunabula, so that texts are available online.

Speaking of online resources, one can access Talmudic manuscripts, wedding contracts, and even ancient maps of Jerusalem. RAMBI is of particular interest. It is an index of Judaica articles in various Israeli journals.

Another project is putting the library's catalogue online, so that it will be available to researchers worldwide. The Hebrew catalogue has been digitalized, as has been done with much of the Latin-character cards (emphasis has been put on Judaica). Cyrillic and Arabic still await computer input. The ephemera collection of materials not regularly published (posters, stickers, handbills, leaflets) has also not yet been put online.

The Judaica reading room has 40,000 open-stack volumes, and it can be difficult to find a seat particularly when yeshivot are on vacation. But, there are other general reading rooms. One covers the Middle East. Another specializes in periodicals. From there one can place orders to see books from the 4.5 million volumes kept in closed stacks.

Gershom Scholem (1897–1982) was not a religious Jew, but he was a renowned scholar of Jewish mysticism and a bibliophile of the first order. Unknown to most people, it was Scholem who developed the expanded Judaica entries in the Dewey decimal cataloguing system used in many libraries today.

This author found the sheet music of a cantor of the early twentieth century, not available elsewhere. Although the pages were published in the United States, he could not find the music in any of the large American libraries.

In 2007 it was decided to separate the National Library from the University Library as part of a long-term project.

The library can be reached by the 9, 19, 24 and 28 busses to Givat Ram. Identification (e.g., identity card, passport) is required to enter the university campus. Entrance to some library reading rooms is restricted to adults. Tours in English or Hebrew can be arranged with advance notice.

Most departments are open Sunday–Thursday 0900–1800, but for specific information it is best to call Tel. 02-658 5027. Closed Friday–Shabbat.

Heichal Shlomo Museum

In prior years Heichal Shlomo on Jerusalem's King George Street was the seat of the Chief Rabbinate and its Religious court. The Rabbinate moved several years ago from the 1950s structure to more modern offices, but Heichal Shlomo is still being put to use. The Wolffson Museum of Jewish Art is expanding its collection and is now on the third floor and has intentions to eventually occupy the entire building.

The museum presents basic Judaism and the art that accompanies it. The first set of exhibits in the museum introduces the visitor to the fundamentals of a synagogue. We pray facing towards Jerusalem, but where is Jerusalem? There is a compass with printed overlay; when the needle points north, a special indicator shows the direction of Jerusalem.

A recreated synagogue has a Torah Ark from Italy, and on display is an exquisite wooden carved Ark with Curtain from Mantua (sixteenth–eighteenth centuries).

A stained glass window showing an artist's rendition of The Temple Mount as seen from the Mount of Olives was saved from the 1969 demolition of the Higher Broughton Synagogue in Manchester.

Tefillin are central to Jewish prayer. As a display shows, the various stages in the making of the black boxes, the parchment, and even bags to hold the tefillin, with and without embroidered names.

There are antiquities in the museum, but not everything is old or unusual. There are unique skull caps, amongst which there is a modern paper skullcap with organizational imprint, typical of what is given to men without head covering entering a synagogue.

A room to the right of the main hall contains traditional objects of holidays, though sometimes with a modern flavor. These include two silver "wagons" used to hold *charoset*, a recently manufactured matzo plate with *"ha lachma anya"* inscribed around a drawing of Egypt, and a very tastefully designed reddish-orange decanter with *"Pesach"* in white letters.

To the left of the main hall another room describes how *Pesach* has been observed on the Israeli kibbutz. Although many of the *haggadahs* are certainly not traditional, it is clear that *Pesach* was still a significant Jewish holiday, even to the non-observant. That exhibit is accompanied by a very cute film in which children act out *"chad gadya."*

Not everything in the museum is joyous. We must never forget the havoc wrecked on the Jewish people by the Nazis. A reminder is a torn and cut Torah scroll and a section of another Torah scroll fitted as a batter head in a drum. (On the much more positive side, the museum also has parts of a fading thirteenth century Torah scroll from Germany.)

The museum contains a reconstruction of the office of Israel's first Ashkenazi Chief Rabbi, Yitzchak HaLevi Herzog (1889–1959).

Although the museum collection is designed for the novice with little Jewish background, an informed Judaica enthusiast should enjoy the visit.

Next to the Great Synagogue on King George Street, Jerusalem. Open Sunday–Thursday, 1000–1400. Closed Shabbat. Tours in English by special arrangement. Entry: Adults NIS 15, children and seniors NIS 10, families NIS 40. Tel. 02-624 7908. Handicapped accessible.

Herzl Center Museum

One cannot shun reality. Theodor Herzl (1860–1904), for better or worse, was a significant figure in Jewish history at the close of the nineteenth and onset of the twentieth centuries. Although Herzl absolutely was not an observant Jew, the man and his work must be understood.

The museum has a four part multi-media presentation, the first three parts of which try to explain Herzl and his deeds, and the fourth casts him as a hero of modern Israel.

Herzl was a product of the Jewish Enlightenment. Born in Budapest in 1860, he had no real Jewish education. He identified himself with the Germanic world of Vienna and its culture. Slowly, he realized that he was a Jew. Government service was problematic. The theater was just as difficult. Herzl tried journalism and moved to cover exploits in Paris, the land of *"liberté, fraternité, égalité."* The Dreyfus Affair totally smashed Herzl's Germanic dream. He had to confront rampant anti-Semitism that haunts the secular Jew no less than the religious Jew. He wrote the *Judenstadt*, his answer to discrimination. It was also the tacit admission that the Enlightenment—Jews fitting into the non-Jewish world—failed.

In a technically effective presentation the museum shows Herzl's keen skills of organization, bringing together in Basle in 1897 Jews from sixteen countries to hear his message of a Jewish State. His words came at the right time. He promulgated an idea that Jews wanted to hear—a safe haven free of anti-Semitism.

If Herzl's skills of organization were excellent, his political understanding was poor. The museum presents a superficial and non-critical explanation of Herzl. He traveled extensively, from prime minister to sultan, looking for someone to approve his charter for a Jewish State. He did not realize that the sultan in Constantinople, the titular ruler of Palestine, was too weak to upset the *status quo*. The Romanoff czar was beset with problems in the Balkans and in the East. The English did have an interest in Palestine, but they wanted to carve a piece of the Ottoman Empire for themselves and not for anyone else.

With the failure of rapid approval for a Jewish State in Palestine, Herzl agreed to "Jewish Uganda." In retrospect, this entire chapter in history is an embarrassment. There are some who try to dismiss it as a temporary refuge from anti-Semitism until a state could be established in Palestine. Others argued that there is no difference if a Jew lives in Uganda, England, or Japan—they are all far from the boundaries of *Eretz Yisrael*.

The museum presentation is candid on one point—Herzl failed in his diplomatic gallivanting. He exhausted his family fortune, but even as an entirely secular Jew he reminded the world of Jews' connection to the Land of Israel.

If the first three parts of the museum try to bring understanding to Herzl, the man, the last part is a blatant effort at building the image of Herzl, the myth. He is cast as a visionary, responsible for the State of Israel and its achievements. In reality he delivered the right message at the right time, but he was totally incapable of putting it into effect.

The time has come, more than one hundred years after the heyday of Herzl, for us to reconsider the man and his place in history. Unfortunately, this museum depicts Herzl as the champion of Zionist lore, rather than bringing a new and critical understanding of a man in his time and a better view of his influence on Jewish history.

The Herzl Museum is on Mt. Herzl, opposite the entrance to Bayit VeGan. The museum is open Sunday–Thursday 0845–1600 (last entry 1515), Friday 0845–1300. Closed Shabbat. An entrance fee of NIS 25 for adults and NIS 20 for children/seniors is charged. Admission must be arranged in advance at telephone 02-632 1515. The general museum office can be reached at 02-632 1500.

The grave of Herzl is near the museum and can be visited without charge.

Israel Museum *(See color plate 29, p. 107)*

In a visit to the Judaica Wing of the Israel Museum one literally walks through hundreds of years of Jewish custom and history.

It is common for Jews to marry during the weeks before Pesach. One item on display is an illustrated pocket-size haggadah (Vienna, 1721) written on vellum. This was a typical wedding gift from the groom to his bride before marriage. What did she typically give to him in return? Also on display is a nineteenth century matzo cover from Poland, with carefully colored hand-embroidery on a white background.

Throughout the centuries there have been Jews who have had difficulty understanding Hebrew. A haggadah printed by letterpress in Venice in 1609 has an answer. Illustrations by woodcut depict parts of the seder with a translation into Judeo-Italian. For those who prefer French, there is a Haggadah printed in Bordeaux in 1813.

A synagogue dedicated in 1700 in Vitorio Venete, northern Italy, was brought to Israel in 1965 and reconstructed in the Israel Museum. The synagogue had been on the second and third floors of a building. Although the shul was used by Ashkenazim, the benches are along the walls as in many Sephardic synagogues, rather than in center rows. An exhibit concerning Jewish women is just where one would expect—in the upper storey women's section.

There are three other reconstructed synagogues in the museum. One is an eighteenth century structure, the Chorev Synagogue from Horb, a small town in southern Germany near Bamberg. The ceiling has exquisite artwork done by Eliezer Sussman, the son of a family from Brody, Galicia. The simple building was used for prayers until 1864, when it was turned into a hay barn. In 1913 local residents discovered the history of the "barn." It was then brought to the Bamberg Museum and was recently transferred to the Israel Museum.

Another reconstructed synagogue is from Cochin in southern India near Kerala. The building dates from 1539–1544 with a women's gallery added in the seventeenth century.

The museum has an excellent collection of havdalah spice boxes. One nineteenth century spice box from Austro-Hungary is in the shape of an apple. Another, made in Vilna in 1863, is in the form of a sunflower. There is a bird atop a tree (eighteenth century, Poland) and even a "locomotive" to hold fragrances (Netherlands, nineteenth century).

The museum is open Monday and Wednesday, 1000–1600; Tuesday 1600–2100; Thursday 1000–2100. Not Shomer Shabbat. Entrance: Adults NIS 42, Students NIS 30, Children NIS 21. Busses 9, 17 from center city

Jerusalem, and the 24/24A. Tour of the Judaica Wing Wednesday 1100. Tel. 02-670 8811. Note: Much of the museum is closed until completion of reconstruction, scheduled for May, 2010.

Miniature of Jerusalem

On 5 July 2006 the miniature of Jerusalem during Second Temple period, housed for forty years outside the Holyland Hotel, opened in its new home at the Israel Museum. The 500:1 model covers a one-half acre lot; it was moved in one thousand pieces over a period of sixty-six days.

After the Miniature was removed, at least fifty Intermediate Bronze Age (approximately 2300–2000 BCE) graves were discovered.

The idea of the model is to give a visual representation of what Jerusalem was like in 66 CE, when the city was at its zenith before the Roman siege. This was not long after Herod sent 10,000 workers to toil more than nine years in refurbishing the Second Temple.

Herod's motivation in building was personal glory and aggrandizement of his name. *Megilat Ta'anit* (Chapters 9, 11) records that the annual anniversary of his death was celebrated with joy.

There are extensive problems in maintaining the miniature. Since the idea of building the model was raised by Hans Kroch (1887-1970) in the 1950s, understanding of the period has greatly changed. During the period of conceptualization and building of the miniature, the Old City was in Jordanian hands. After 1967 archeological excavations yielded new light on life in the city two thousand years ago.

The overall impression that the miniature leaves is positive. It gives good perspective to the city. The lower city was poor; wealth was abundant in the upper city. Herod expanded the limits of Jerusalem by building new walls; most of the area that he added was strategically superfluous and sparsely populated. The Antonia, a fortress meant to guard the Temple Mount, was both large and impressive (though it was destined to be obliterated by Roman soldiers). And, central to the city was the Second Temple, geographically on the side, but the focal point of community life.

An important part of the presentation is the pathway around the model from which one can see the city from all directions. One enters as though he were standing on the Mount of Olives. Signs indicate other vantage points.

There is "license" in how and where some buildings are built. The red roofs of upper city buildings are not substantiated by archeological findings. Sources state that there was a Roman theater even in the period before the Destruction of the Second Temple, yet there is no evidence that it was located as shown in the miniature.

Perhaps the most bothersome detail in the miniature is the representation of Hulda Gates on the southern wall of the Temple Mount. They are shown as two pairs of two gates. Religious sources and now archeological excavations show clearly that such was not the case. There was one entrance gate and more gates for exit.

Problems with fine details should not prevent visitors from visiting the model, which is not meant to be a text-book lesson in ancient architecture. Its purpose is to convey the nature and spirit of first century Jerusalem, and that it does very well.

Shrine of the Book

The story of how most of the scrolls came to the Israel Museum is unusual. They were found in a cave overlooking the Dead Sea by a Bedouin shepherd tending his flock in 1947. Some of the scrolls were bought by Jews. Others were acquired by Arabs, who eventually kept the ancient writings in the Palestine Archeology Museum (now the Rockefeller Museum) in East Jerusalem. From 1952 through 1956 Jordanian search teams found scrolls in ten more caves.

By the 1960s it became apparent that the scrolls were of significant historical importance and public interest. As a result the Jordanians put some of their scrolls on display at the 1964–1965 New York World's Fair and again at Expo '67 in Montréal.

Political events influenced the future of the scrolls. In October 1966 the Palestine Archeology Museum was nationalized by the Jordanians, and a decision was made to transfer the scrolls held there to the national museum in Amman. The scrolls were carefully packed and were ready for shipment. Then, the Six Day War interrupted the transfer.

On 7 June 1967, two hours after Israeli forces entered East Jerusalem, two Jordanian archeologists secretly entered the besieged Palestine Archeology Museum, grabbed the "Copper Scroll," and eventually brought it to Amman. That scroll, written in sixty-four lines on a thin sheet of copper, was discovered in 1952. It described the location of sizeable material wealth (gold and silver)—never found by people looking to get rich quickly.

As to the scrolls in Israel, they were placed on display in the Shrine of the Book at the Israel Museum, which opened in 1965. The Shrine was considered an architectural landmark, but the events of 1967 quickly made it too small. There were too many scrolls after the scrolls at the Palestine Archeology Museum fell into Israeli hands. They remained there until 2001–2002, when they were moved to a vault belonging to the Israel Antiquities Authority at the Israel Museum.

Recently, the Israel Museum decided to invest in the Dead Sea scrolls display. A Dead Sea Scrolls Research Center has been opened, combining presentation of the material with an auditorium and learning center to host seminars. One of the projects is to develop online digital access to the Dead Sea treasures. Another project is a fictional film that tries to depict the human side of the Dead Sea community and the tensions between it and Jews of Jerusalem.

From a religious perspective, perhaps the most significant of the Dead Sea scrolls is the Isaiah Scroll, copied down by a scribe in the latter years of the Second Temple and containing essentially the entire book of Isaiah. That scroll has been one of the first projects of the research center. Although pictures of the scroll were published in the 1960s, new photographic techniques have significantly improved poorly seen parts of the scroll.

The Dead Sea community was not very large with most estimates ranging between 40 and 150 people. The absolute maximum appears to be 200. In realistic terms, the significant events of the last years of the Second Temple took place in Jerusalem. The Dead Sea community was at best a "side show." But, the written legacy that was left behind at the Dead Sea has staked out a piece of history for that community.

Entrance to the Jerusalem Miniature and the Shrine of the Book are included in the general fee to visit the Israel Museum.

Italian Jewry *(See color plate 30, p. 107)*

The Museum of Italian Jewry is tucked away on the second floor of the former Schmidt Compound at Rechov Hillel 27. The collection has unique items, even in a city like Jerusalem that abounds in displays of Judaica.

The compound was named after Wilhelm Schmidt (1868-1954), head of the German Catholic Society in Palestine during the late nineteenth and early twentieth centuries. The compound started as a German Catholic monastery, a school for women of Syrian-Christian descent, and as a residence for Christian pilgrims. During the 1940s the society, popularly known as the Schmidt Girls' School, moved to its current quarters outside the Damascus Gate. The Italian Jews moved into the compound in 1952.

The focal point of the museum is the Conegliano Veneto Synagogue, built in 1701 in a small town between the cities of Venice and Padua. The last services were held in the synagogue in 1918 after Conegliano was conquered by Austro-Hungarian troops; their chaplain brought Jewish soldiers into the synagogue for Yom Kippur prayers. The synagogue then stood empty until 1951, when the building was carefully taken apart and reassembled at its current site. Today, Jews observing the Italian rite of prayer assemble to pray every Shabbat in the atmosphere of "The Old Country," just as it was three hundred years ago. Many of the benches, the chandeliers, and the pulpit are original to the building, as is the Ark, dating back to 1652.

In the rooms next to the synagogue there are two *kiddush* cups with covers, so that nothing will fall into the wine after it is poured. An eighteenth century circumcision "kit" is housed in an elegant carrying case (implements made by a Christian silversmith due to the papal prohibition forbidding Jews from manufacturing items in silver and gold). Matzo baking equipment fills one show case, and the museum also boasts what is thought to be the oldest known *parochet*, dating to 1342.

The panels of a late eighteenth century *succah* once owned by the Sullam family of Venice depict scenes related to the Exodus, including the Egyptians, horse and rider, drowning in the sea. In the background the designing artist drew the dry land from which Pharaoh witnessed the debacle of his army. A good look at that background yields buildings reminiscent of the artist's own background—the buildings of Venice!

Thirty to forty-five minutes should be allotted to the museum visit; guided visits on Thursday take longer. To enrich the experience it is recommended that one read a summary of Italian Jewish history before coming to the museum.

Rechov Hillel 27. Sunday, Tuesday, Wednesday 0900–1700; Monday 0900–1400; Thursday, Friday 0900–1300. Part of the museum is open as a functioning synagogue on Shabbat. Entrance fee: Adults NIS 15; students and seniors NIS 10. An additional fee is charged for weekday tours. Tel. 02-624 1610.

Jerusalem Mall (Malcha)

The shopping mall was opened in 1993 and contains 260 shops including 30 kosher restaurants and cafés of which several are *Mehadrin* (most of the fast food variety). Although frequented by many of the ultra-orthodox, the majority of clothing stores clearly caters to the non-religious.

There is one item of particular interest in the Mall; in the synagogue there is a classical *Aron Kodesh* on loan from the Museum of Italian Jewry.

In the nearby neighborhood there are several Canaanite and Roman era graves.

Open Sunday–Thursday 0930–2200, Friday 0900–1500, Saturday from one hour after Shabbat until 2300. Buses 4, 5, 6, 12, 17, 18, 24, 31. The mall is close to the Jerusalem train station. Tel. 02-679 1333.

Knesset *(See color plate 31, p. 108)*

The first *Knesset* in Jerusalem was on Rechov King George in a building now occupied by rabbinic courts. The interior has been redesigned, and there is nothing to attract a tourist.

The current building was completed in August, 1966. The entrance gate was designed by David Palombo (1920–1966), who also sculpted the entrance to the Hall of Remembrance at Yad VaShem; a museum in his former studio is located on Mt. Zion. Inside, one can see the wall hanging and mosaics designed by Marc Chagall.

Opposite the *Knesset* entrance to the west are the Rose Garden and a Menorah designed by Beno Elkon and donated to the new State of Israel by the British government. The Menorah shows twenty-nine events in Jewish history.

There are two common methods of visiting the Knesset: Tours in English are available Sunday and Thursday between 0830, 1200 and 1345; reservations should be made at telephones 02-675 3420 or 02-675 3416. Alternatively, when the Knesset is in session, the public gallery is open Monday and Tuesday at 1600 and Wednesday at 1100.

Presentation of an Israeli identification card or foreign passport is required. A strict dress code is enforced.

Machane Yehudah

Market

Machne Yehuda Market. Early in the morning before the stalls open

Machane Yehudah was founded by Sephardic Jews, directed by Joseph Navon (1858-1934), a native Jerusalemite who served as the Portuguese Consul an was instrumental in building the Jerusalem-Jaffa railroad.

The area took on the nature of a market as early as Ottoman days, since it offered a convenient location to sell fruits and vegetables. The British tried to shut down the market, but its tradition was already well entrenched. When they saw that what they considered unsanitary could not be uprooted, they allowed the building of eighty-one stores in 1931. Years later Israel tried to close the market, but with the same unsuccessful results. The area was then cleaned up, a roof was built over part of the market, and lighting/electricity was improved.

Today this area is the city's retail produce market. One can find a seemingly endless supply of fresh fruits and vegetables under various rabbinical certifications. There is also a smattering of bakeries and vendors of delicacies such as fish (fresh, smoked, pickled, etc.).

Restaurants of various qualities can be found along Rechov Agrippas, behind the "shuk" (Hebrew for "market") and parallel to Jaffa Road.

Machane Yehudah is not a typical tourist site. It is an experience. It's a place to buy something to eat—from a piece of fruit to an entire meal—and to enjoy the hustle and bustle of the market.

Stores begin to open 0700–0730. By 0900 sales are in full swing. Most stores close at 1900, but some are open later. The *shuk* is busiest on Thursdays and Friday mornings and on the eves of holidays. Prices are slashed dramatically during the last hour before Shabbat as stores close.

Ministry of Health

Several buildings away from Zohorei Hama is a not-so-well kept structure that houses district offices of the Ministry of Health. The building is notable for its imposing stone entrance with iron gates. It is there that inoculations are given for travelers going abroad.

The building was constructed as a wedding gift in 1882 for the son of a well-to-do Christian Arab family. The groom, however, passed away just hours before the wedding. Word spread that an evil spirit haunted the building; hence, it sat on the market unsold, until the Ottoman rulers of Jerusalem turned the edifice into a hospital. An Ottoman symbol can still be seen over the entrance way.

Zohorei Hama – Sun Dial Synagogue
(See color plate 32, p. 108)

This synagogue, constructed in 1907–1908 by Shmuel Levi, a Russian Jew living in the United States, is located across Rechov Yafo from the Machane Yehudah market. Levi had purchased the land two years previously. The first upper floors constituted a hostel; the ground storey held a synagogue, still in use today.

A noteworthy part of the building is a five meter (sixteen foot) semicircular sundial constructed by Moshe Shapira. Smaller sundials were put in place to serve as backups, and two regular clocks, one on European time and one on the "Eretz Yisrael time," were for cloudy days. Shapira, a renowned engineer who learned the art of constructing sundials from religious literature, was later asked to build a sundial on the Temple Mount. As a devout Jew he had serious questions, including the prohibition to set foot on the Temple Mount. Much to the disappointment and ire of the Moslems, Shapira declined the request. He then had to flee Jerusalem for his safety. He never was able to return.

The building was seriously damaged by fire in 1941, then restored in 1980. It is from this edifice that the funeral eulogies for Rabbi Moshe Feinstein were conducted.

Today this is one of the "minyan factories" of Jerusalem. The Sephardic prayer rite is observed.

Mandate Prison

The rope still swings from the gallows, a chilling reminder of the fifteen Jews hanged by the British during their rule over Mandate Palestine. The cells in which prisoners spent their last night have been refurbished, and the solitary cells have been restored. Now the Central Jerusalem Prison is a museum run by the Ministry of Defense in testimony to the thousands who were imprisoned here.

The building, in the heart of Jerusalem in the Russian Compound, was designed by Martin Ivanovich Efinger and built from 1860 until 1864 by the *Imperial Orthodox Palestine Society* to serve the large numbers of Russian pilgrims to Jerusalem. The compound included a mission, consulate, hospital, and hostels. The Russian Compound comprises almost seventeen acres including structures on Rechov Helena HaMalka, as well as a court of justice, church, police station, the Duhovnia Russian Mission building, and a large office building, as well as the Mandate Prison.

Mandate Prison. Gallows

The Mandate Prison was constructed as the Elizabeth Feodorovna Hostel for Women, housing Christian pilgrims, until 1917, when the newly arrived British converted it into the prison.

One of the most famous people associated with the prison was not an inmate. It was Rabbi Aryeh Levine (1885–1969), who visited inmates virtually every Shabbat and Yom Tov from 1924 until the facility was closed in 1948. He would shake the hands of the prisoners, and then pray with them. Weather never stopped the Rabbi.

Monetary gain also did not interest Rabbi Levine. When he was offered the official position of prison rabbi, he declined. His was a task of kindness without financial reimbursement. (Rabbi Yaacov Goldman, then a South African officer in the British Army, accepted the job. He enjoyed very cordial relations with Levine. After 1948 he stayed in Israel and became the secretary of Chief Rabbi Herzog.)

Where did Rabbi Levine pray in the prison? In Cell 29, which was converted into a synagogue replete with Torah Scroll (for many years kept under lock and key by an Arab prisoner). The synagogue-in-prison also had a long-term sexton, Yehudah Feder, a Lehi (also known as the Stern Gang after the founder, Avraham Stern) member incarcerated on illegal weapons charges. Later Feder would become the deputy director-general of the Israel Ministry of Health.

The British were very tolerant of religion in the prison. According to the Palestine Ordinance of 1933 (revised 1946), inmates were entitled to a place or room to pray. Hence Cell 29 was set aside for a synagogue. Clergy could visit, so Rabbi Levine was allowed in without question. There was even a separate kitchen that supplied kosher food to the Jewish inmates.

There were unique ways in which Jewish inmates coped with imprisonment. At one stage Dr. Souriano, a Jewish physician, toured the kosher kitchen and was appalled to find small eggs from young chickens being served. A solution had to be found. He consulted with Rabbi Levine, who came up with the innovative rabbinic decision that the eggs did not meet kosher requirements. Only eggs with a stamp from the Jewish cooperative could be trusted! The British felt they had no choice, and ordered eggs from the Jewish company. The British could ask for smaller eggs, but only larger eggs were sent.

Public prayer was permitted only on Shabbat and holidays. One year the warden decided that since Tisha B'Av was not an official holiday, Jews could not gather in the synagogue. They would have to keep a regular work schedule. The Jewish answer was adamant. They would declare a hunger strike! (The British apparently never asked what a hunger strike was on a fast day!) In a panic the warden summoned Rabbi Levine, who again came up with a rabbinic decision. Of course this is a holiday, and Jews could not work. The warden, hearing the response of the Rabbi, permitted prayer in the synagogue.

Rabbi Levine was an unusual man. He entered the prison through the small door used by inmates, and he would sit in synagogue as though he were just another one of the crowd. Prisoners would place notes in his pockets. During the week he would bring the notes to families, and the next Shabbat he would often come back with responses. When he found that one prisoner had no family to visit him, the Rabbi found someone to come regularly to see the prisoner.

The rugs that served as mattresses in the prison are still on the floor. Uniforms are still on the clothing hooks. And Cell 23, the Jews-only cell opposite the synagogue, can be visited. There, Jews dug a tunnel to connect to the sewage system, thus escaping from the prison. But what did they do with the dirt removed from the tunnel? Again, a solution was found. They complained to the warden that it was difficult to wash the floor of the cell. There was nowhere to dispose of the water. Could they dig a pool? The request was granted. No one noticed that the prisoners added dirt from the tunnel to dirt from the pool.

There were numerous cases of escape. Yaacov Eliav (1917–1985) of Lehi was imprisoned in the Russian Compound. Warden Carlton invited Eliav to his house next to the prison to do electrical work. Eliav asked Carlton to hold wires to the ceiling since it was dangerous to leave them on the floor, then he dashed out an open window. But, where could Eliav go? He ran to nearby Mea Shearim into the house of a Chassid, whom he did not know. Certainly a religious Jew would not turn him over to non-Jews. Shortly afterwards Eliav emerged from the house wearing Chassidic garb and strolled to freedom.

The museum is open Sunday–Thursday 0800–1600. Closed Friday–Shabbat. Entry NIS 10 for visitors 18–65 years of age; NIS 5 for children and seniors. Tel. 02-623 3166. Guided tours (highly recommended) by prior arrangement.

Mea Shearim *(See color plate 33, p. 108)*

Today Mea Shearim is touted as the epitome of a religious Jerusalem neighborhood, but it hardly started out that way. Conrad Schick conceived the idea of Mea Shearim in 1846. Joseph Rivlin was involved in the planning. A Christian Arab from Bethlehem was the primary contractor.

The name of the neighborhood does not mean "one hundred gates" (a modern mis-translation). It is based upon a blessing to Isaac (Genesis 26:12) that produce reaped would increase one hundred fold.

The neighborhood grew rapidly from its inception in 1874, based upon a model set up by Schick. By 1880 the empty fields of the early 1870s contained one hundred buildings. Twenty years later that number had tripled.

The original idea of wide open spaces became an historical memory, as buildings crowded one near the other. Originally the idea was to build groups of buildings around an inner courtyard, but the demand for land quickly revised the concept. Cow sheds were built. There was pressure from the light industry. Even Israel's longest existing bakery was located in Mea Shearim; Yehoshua Berman bought a flour mill from Moshe Leib Friedlander several years after the neighborhood began, and then he moved his bakery next to the mill. The Berman Bakery (founded 1875) remained in Mea Shearim until it moved to its current location in Givat Shaul in 1965.

Batei Ungaren is an adjacent area that has been absorbed into Mea Shearim. It is an enclosed area of four hundred small apartments (typical for general housing during that era) built in 1891 under the auspices of the Austrian consul. Its ultra-orthodox population maintains a strictly religious lifestyle.

It was only in the early twentieth century that Mea Shearim began to take on its current ultra-Orthodox character. The trend of increasing ultra-Orthodoxy was intensified, when many refugees from the fallen Jewish Quarter moved there in 1948.

Mekor Baruch

This neighborhood, adjacent to Geula, also traces its origins to the Schneller Woods. Similar to Geula, it has been transformed from an essentially secular and Mizrachi area to an ultra-Orthodox center.

The neighborhood was founded by Rabbi Baruch Aharonov of the United States in 1923. Its distinguishing architectural quality was the predominance of three story homes. A Neighborhood Council began in 1933, and after the establishment of the State of Israel, Mekor Baruch housed many immigrants from Morocco and Kurdistan. For many years neighborhood activities were centered on the Tachkemoni (Mizrachi) school, established in 1929. Another previous landmark was Machon Gold, a post-high school seminary for the Diaspora established in 1958, which closed in 2008.

Motza *(See color plate 34, p. 108)*

For many travelers Motza is best known as the area next to the sharp curve in the highway just before the ascent to Jerusalem. Motza, however, is mentioned twice in the Bible, and very prominently in the Mishna (Succah 4:5) as a source of *aravot* that were used in the Temple.

A decision was taken to straighten the highway with a bypass that was to have been built in 2003 to avoid the curve, the scene of endless traffic accidents. The bypass construction, however, was delayed when construction uncovered agricultural storage rooms from the late Second Temple period.

"Motza," is known from an inscription on an eighth century BCE earthenware vessel discovered in northern Jerusalem.

Do not be fooled by today's road that passes through Motza. The curve has been there for centuries, but the highway along its current route dates only to 1942. From Roman times travelers descended from the Kastel on a winding path, then started the two hour trek from the curve to the Old City on a dirt road with a steep incline inside the Jerusalem forest.

As early as Byzantine times there was a church and pilgrims' hospice in Motza. Today the foundation of the Byzantine building serves as a catering hall on the floor below a synagogue (technically several meters outside the current Jerusalem city limits).

Over the years a new church was built in Motza during the Crusader period by pilgrims who mistakenly thought they had found the valley in which David had confronted Goliath.

It was only in 1860 that Jews returned to Motza, a daring step so far from the protection of the Old City walls. Members of the Yehudah and Yellin families started acquiring land and water rights in the area for the purpose of farming, but from the very beginning there were problems. Neither was an Ottoman citizen, so they were forbidden by law to purchase land. Five years later cutouts were found, and the lands were officially transferred to Jewish hands.

Yehoshua Yellin (1843-1924) was quick to appreciate business potential. In 1869 the Ottomans began to pave the Jaffa-Jerusalem road for use by buggies. By 1871 Yellin built a second storey above the Byzantine ruins and opened a café and small hotel for travelers who feared they might reach Jerusalem after nightfall, when the city gates were locked. In the other direction there were those who left Jerusalem in the afternoon, stayed over-night in Yellin's hotel, and made an early morning start for Ramla and Jaffa.

Motza boasts of an important "first" in modern Israeli history. In 1880–81 Yellin and a partner opened a short-lived roof-tile factory, the first major Jewish industry outside the Old City.

During the Ottoman period Motza was known as Kolonia, a quiet Arab village. In 1929 Arabs from Kolonia participated in the murderous anti-Jewish riots; they slaughtered some of the Jewish residents. The Arab village was evacuated in 1948 and leveled in 1955. Portions of several buildings still remain, more as an historical curiosity than important structures.

In the early 1890s Yehoshua Yellin built a house for himself behind the hotel, which he sold. The location was perfect, with a deep well in the courtyard. That residence is now being restored, and will hopefully be inaugurated as a local history museum.

The history of the hotel took interesting turns. In the first years of the twentieth century four families shared the building as a residence. In 1917 the Cohen family moved in, and separated rooms for a hotel, school and synagogue. The hotel, though, was a victim of technology, when motor vehicles were introduced in 1922, and it was no longer necessary to rest animals and travelers in Motza. In 1948 the building was used as an earthenware factory. Then in 1961 a major change took place. Two religious Jews decided to restore the building to its historic use. Once again the hotel with a Byzantine foundation became a synagogue. It was realized that praying in someone's house was not a long-range solution. Since that time the synagogue has been renovated.

Museum on the Seam *(See color plate 35, p. 108)*

The Museum on the Seam, housed in the building once used by Israeli security forces manning the Mandelbaum Gate crossing (named for the house of Simcha Mandelbaum, a Karliner chassid) to Jordanian Jerusalem, was constructed in 1924 by the Baramki family. At one point the building contained a museum dedicated to the War of Independence and the fight for Jerusalem. The presentation was dull and uninspiring, hence there were few visitors. In 1995 it was decided to open a new museum, which was inaugurated in 1999 under the direction of Rafael Etgar (1947-), an Israeli artist who trained in the Bezalael Institute and has taught in prominent schools abroad. That museum is dedicated to socio-political issues that concern Israel today, and not surprising given Etgar's background, the medium is art.

One exhibition dealt with violence and gives a good idea about the nature of the museum. It was not an exhibition dedicated to history. It was a display meant to evoke thought, and it did that very successfully.

It is difficult for a person to go through the museum without a guide. There are exhibits with explanations (in Hebrew and English), but more is gained when someone raises issues and tries to have the visitor answer. No, not just answer. The point is that the visitor must think and examine his own self. To describe the museum in religious terminology, the exhibitions are an attempt for each person to examine his own personal traits.

One should not feel out of place at the museum. Many visitors are soldiers, policemen, and students. International tourists come, as do a few Palestinians. There are also ultra-Orthodox Jews from the neighboring Mea Shearim area. The exhibit affords all of us the opportunity to think about our attitudes and values.

The museum is at R. HaHandasah 4. Open Sunday–Thursday 0900–1700; Friday 0900–1400. Closed Shabbat. Admission: Adults NIS 25, Students NIS 20, Senior citizens and Handicapped NIS 10; children under fourteen not admitted. Busses: 6, 15, 23, 30. Allow forty-five minutes to one hour for visit without guide; longer with guide. Tel. 02-628 1278.

Natural History Museum

The grounds are impressive. The building, a nineteenth century Arab mansion, was imposing in its day. The house and grounds were taken over as the residence of the Ottoman Governor, then after World War I the British Governor moved in. Later during the Mandate, the building served as an officers' club. After the War of Independence the structure was abandoned until groups started to use it for nature studies. Finally, the Natural History Museum was opened in 1962. One has the distinct impression, however, that little has changed in the exhibits since then.

The museum exhibits are labeled in Hebrew, with occasional English translation of floral or animal names. Although guided tours are offered for groups, the individual visitor is left to fend for himself.

There are interesting facts that one can learn from the exhibits. Syrian brown bears ceased to exist in Israel in the nineteenth century. Crocodiles (*crocodylus niloticus*) disappeared in the twentieth century. These tidbits, however, are overshadowed by an endorsement of evolution that taints the reliability of information presented.

Neither does the exhibit generate confidence in the information presented. An article from *Yediot Aharonot* about dinosaur remains in Oklahoma bears no date or page number. Another exhibit talks about evidence recovered in Mitzpe Ramon showing the existence of pre-historic reptiles, but that "evidence" is not properly specified.

This museum is not recommended unless you have a very specific interest in natural history. Even then the exhibit should be viewed with due scrutiny.

Rechov Mohliver 6. Busses 4, 18. Sunday, Tuesday, Thursday 0900–1330; Monday, Wednesday 0900–1800. Chol HaMoed 0900–1500. Open Shabbat. Library is open Monday, Wednesday 1500–1800. Fee: Adults NIS 15, Children 0-18 NIS 12. No strollers allowed. Not wheelchair accessible. Tel. 02-563 1116.

North African Jewry *(See color plate 36, p. 109)*

The neighborhood around Rechov HaMaaravim is often called by the Arabic name, "Mamila," but for old Jerusalemites the maze of winding walkways is *Machane Yisrael*, the first neighborhood outside the Old City to be developed by Jews residing in Jerusalem.

In 1854 Rabbi David ben Shimon (1822-1879), also known by the acronym Radba"sh, came to Palestine after a long overland journey from Rabat. He is particularly renowned for his responsa on Talmud Tractate *Gittin* (Divorce). Soon he was followed to Jerusalem by his students, who became the seeds of a "Moroccan Community," separate from other Sephardim. Six years later the Radba"sh started to interest Moroccan Jews from the Old City in moving to a new area, and several years after that they started building *Machane Yisrael*. First to be constructed were houses and a synagogue. In 1870 the Radba"sh opened a Kollel in the neighborhood.

At first the neighborhood flourished. By 1897 some 150 Moroccan families lived in the growing sprawl of new houses. By the outbreak of World War I, two buildings had been constructed from charity collections to house the community's indigent.

Times changed. Ottoman rule was replaced by the British Mandate, and troubles flared between Jews and Arabs. *Machane Yisrael*, sandwiched between Arab neighborhoods and a Waqf (Supreme Moslem Council) cemetery with graves dating to the Mamluk period, became a problematic if not dangerous place to live. Some efforts were made in the 1930s to maintain the houses, but *Machane Yisrael* deteriorated, and in 1959 a serious proposal was put forward to raze the neighborhood.

Fortunately, preservationists eventually won out in favor of restoration. In 1988 the last tenants left the dilapidated building that once had been the home to the local *kollel*. There, at Rechov HaMaaravim 13, the World Center for the Heritage of North African Jewry started to build its new home in 1998.

Despite the pretense of North African Jewry, the museum unsurprisingly concentrates on Morocco. Entering the restored building is to leave modern Jerusalem and walk into the ambiance of traditional Morocco. Exquisite carvings support a modern recreation of Moroccan architecture. Decorative pottery and mosaics with Moroccan motifs help set the mood. A highlight is a recreated family salon on the second floor. As the visitor stands in the central patio, it is not difficult for him to imagine himself back in Morocco.

The Center prides itself on being a "living museum." Moroccan culture is thriving in Israel, and the Center is part of that vitality. Lectures are held often, and a special effort is being made to keep alive the Moroccan tradition of liturgical poetry.

The Center is far from finished. Many walls are covered with pictures, but the captions are lacking. Descriptions of the pottery on display also need additional explanation. A room has been set aside as a synagogue, however it is far from completion. As we all know, work based upon donations is often slower than what one would ideally want.

A permanent exhibit on the third floor features vignettes of key figures in Moroccan Jewish history. Accompanying text is in French and Hebrew. This material is also available in a book published by the museum.

Open Sunday–Thursday 0900–1400. Closed Shabbat. NIS 10. Tel. 02- 623 5811.

Note: Not far from the museum, at the corner of Rechov Agron and Rechov HaMelech David is the former Palace Hotel, scheduled to open after refurbishing as a Waldorf-Astoria. The Palace Hotel was built under the auspices of the Supreme Moslem Council and completed in 1929. Two Jewish architects, Tuvia Donia (brother-in-law of Chaim Weizmann) and Baruch Katinka (Haganah member) were responsible for designing the magnificent building. The Peel Commission on Palestine met in the hotel, and it was Katinka who managed to bug the rooms in which the meetings were held. The Haganah also used this unlikely site to secretly store weapons. The building eventually housed Israel government offices. Today the interior with its spiral staircases has been entirely gutted as part of renovations. Only the exterior façade remains.

Otzar HaPoskim *(See color plate 37, p. 109)*

When the enormity of the Holocaust first became apparent in 1944, rabbis immediately realized that they needed tools to begin tackling the problem of potential *agunot*. Rabbi Shmuel Kipnis was assigned the task of setting up Otzar HaPoskim, a repository of rabbinic responsa initially concentrating on married women whose husbands could not give a divorce (*Even HaEzer* 17). What was once a catalogue of over one million index cards with abstracts of questions and answers is now an even more extensive computerized data base, supported by an extensive collection of books on-shelf encompassing the gamut of questions posed to rabbis.

Twenty-one volumes of responsa have been published, but Otzar HaPoskim now has its collection of responsa on CDs; soon a greatly expanded version will be sold on hard disk. The responsa come from more than five thousand books, as well as from journals and decisions of rabbinic courts.

Have a question? You can ask Otzar HaPoskim. An answer, under the trusted rabbinic authority of Rabbi Binyamin Adler, will be forthcoming within a week in Hebrew, Yiddish or English. Answers are in the language of the question asked. Many questions have to do with sensitive family matters, saving the person asking the possible embarrassment of sharing his personal situation with his family rabbi. But not all questions involve privacy and family problems. One question on record is whether an Ashkenazi house owner fulfills requirements with a Sephardic *mezuzah*.

Many rabbinic judges and university students pose a different type of question to Otzar HaPoskim. They are not looking for a specific answer. Rather, they want bibliographic assistance—what are the sources for a particular topic. The library can provide not only a comprehensive list of responsa; it can also send a reasonable number of faxes with the full text of difficult-to-find answers.

Visitors to Otzar HaPoskim are welcomed, and can use the library. A tour with full explanation of the operation is also provided, but advance notice is required.

One prominent rabbi from England searched in other libraries, but found no material regarding Purim in Jericho. Is it the fourteenth or the fifteenth of Adar? He was pessimistic about finding something, but thought that he would try anyway. He was surprised to be given four responsa on the subject.

Otzar HaPoskim has greatly expanded its publishing program. For rabbinic scribes who write bills of divorce, they have a dictionary of 35,000 names, covering all possible spelling variations. There is a newly annotated edition of *Machzor Vitri*, and even a two volume guide to *yibum* (levirite marriage) and *chalitza*. The bookstore is both online and open to visitors on the lower floor of the Otzar HaPoskim office.

Rechov Torah MiTziyon 3 (just beyond the traffic circle behind the Central Bus Station), Jerusalem. Hours: 0830–2030. Tours by appointment. Tel. 02-538 2515.

Promenade

A network of three inter-connected promenades dominates a hillside in East Talpiyot (Armon Hanetziv—the residence of the [British] High Commissioner).

The central Haas Promenade, built over the remnants of a Second Temple era aqueduct, was designed by Lawrence Halprin (1916-2009 and Shlomo Aronson.

The Sherover Promenade was also designed by Aronson. The Goldman Promenade was by Lawrence Halprin and Bruce Levin. Halprin, a well known landscape designer, spent his teenage years in Mandate Palestine.

The view of Jerusalem to the north is breath-taking, but if you are unfamiliar with the city and its landmarks, it is best to visit the Promenade with a guide, who can also show remnants of the ancient aquaduct. Highlights are views of the Mount of Olives, the Temple Mount, and the City of David.

Promenade in Armon Hanetziv. Roman period aquaduct and water tunnel near Promenade

Psalms Museum

Next to the House of Rabbi Kook is an art gallery, the Museum of Psalms, where Moshe Tzvi Berger has on display 150 paintings, each inspired by a chapter of Psalms. The gallery was established in 1995 with the encouragement of Rav Mayer Yehudah Getz, then Rabbi of the Western Wall. A short tour of the collection with Berger is recommended and is best arranged with advance notice. Also of note is the spacious apartment in which the paintings are housed.

Rechov Rabbi Kook 9. Open Sunday–Thursday, 1000–1700. Closed Friday–Shabbat. Entrance is *gratis*, but a donation of NIS 10 is suggested. Tel. 02-623 0025.

Rav Kook House *(See color plate 38, p. 109)*

Rabbi Avraham Yitzchak HaCohen Kook was probably one of the most unique personalities of modern Jewish history. Born in Griva, Latvia in 1865, he received a traditional Jewish education. In 1884 he entered the Volozhin Yeshiva, and in his less than two years there became close to the head of the *yeshiva*, Rabbi Naftali Zvi Yehudah Berlin (commonly known as the *Netziv*) (1817–1893). In 1895 he became the *Rav* of Bausk.

Rabbi Kook soon bolted from the stereotype and established himself as a very unusual personality. He was a staunch supporter of exactness in Jewish Law, but his concerns went well beyond those of a traditional rabbi. He was a mystic. He was a Zionist. He was a pragmatist. And he cherished his fellow man. He shunned wealth. Perhaps best summed up, he was a spiritualist. In 1904 Rabbi Kook made his way to Ottoman Palestine, where he became the Chief Rabbi of Jaffa, a post that included responsibility for agricultural lands in the area. To common amazement, he gave a speech in fluent Hebrew upon assuming his new position.

Not everything can be planned. In 1914 Rabbi Kook traveled to attend the Agudat Yisrael convention in Berlin, but with the outbreak of war he was unable to return to Palestine. After staying two years in Switzerland, Rabbi Kook made his way to London, where he served as rabbi of Machzikei HaDas until his return to Palestine in 1919. During his time in England, he played a significant role in lobbying for the adoption of the Balfour Declaration.

In Palestine a new position awaited Rabbi Kook. He was appointed Chief Rabbi of Jerusalem. Then, two years later Rabbi Kook became the first Ashkenazi Chief Rabbi of Palestine. Two years subsequently an apartment at today's Rechov Rabbi Kook 9 was ready for its new resident. That apartment is now open to the public as a museum.

The building, constructed in the late nineteenth century, bridged the geographic gap between Nachalat Shiva and Mea Shearim. The neighborhood of ten apartments surrounded by a wall was called Beit David, after its philanthropic founder, David Reis. Although it is now less than a block from the traffic of Jaffa Road, then times were different. The area was desolate and rampant with marauders and bandits, so the gate of the surrounding wall was kept locked at night. In 1922–3 a second storey wing was added to part of the residential complex. That became the apartment of Rabbi Kook. As befits a chief rabbi, the apartment had one very unique feature—it contained a private *mikvah*.

Rabbi Kook was a frugal man who balked at materialism. His simple apartment exemplified that approach to life. His office was a modest room big enough to seat only three or four people. In 1924 he transformed the largest room into a *yeshiva*, the precursor of today's *Mercaz Rabbi*. The curriculum of learning reflected his ideas of education. Studying just Talmud is insufficient. Emphasis must also be put on other subjects such as Bible.

(Rabbi Kook took an active role in the ceremony opening Hebrew University in 1925, but in later years he became dismayed at the university's straying from Jewish learning.)

Much misunderstanding surrounds the legacy of Rabbi Kook. He believed in maintaining warmth and friendship towards secularists, but he explicitly rejected their views. His belief in Eretz Yisrael was unswerving, and he is often touted as a leader of religious Zionism. He looked forward to the end of the Diaspora, and to the reestablishment of Jews in their land. Yet, he had severe doubts about the religious Zionist movement. He feared that adherence to the popular tenets of religious Zionism would in the long run strengthen secular Zionism.

Rabbi Kook is mistakenly known for the *heter mechirah* (sale of the land) during *shmitah*. He fervently advocated tithing and strict observance of *shmitah*, but the economic situation of 1910 posed enormous difficulties for the *Yishuv*. The Ottoman Empire was crumbling, and hunger was rampant. Jewish agricultural production could not keep pace with the need for food. Faced with a real threat of starvation, Rabbi Kook declared permission for *heter mechirah*. No, Jews should not simply eat from the year's produce as a measure of saving lives. They should use *heter mechirah*, so as not to forget *shmitah*. Very clearly, his rabbinic decision was valid only for that one year and not a general policy.

The rabbi passed away in 1935 and was succeeded as head of the *yeshiva* by his son, Zvi Yehudah (1891–1982), who solidified the link between *Mercaz HaRav Yeshiva* and the Mizrachi religious Zionist movement. It is through that action that Rabbi Avraham Yitzchak HaCohen Kook posthumously became a champion of Mizrachi Jews.

The House of Rabbi Kook gives good insight into the rabbi. The former *beit midrash* is now used to screen a film about his life (English sound track available on request). Another room houses his archives, including some 50,000 items, which can be used by serious researchers upon prior arrangement.

Rechov Rabbi Kook 9. Open Sunday–Thursday, 0900–1500, Friday and holidays eves 0900–1200. Closed Shabbat. Guided tours of the apartment are available only to groups. Tel. 02-623 2560.

Rebbe's Museum *(See color plate 39, p. 110)*

Walking into the apartment of Mordechai Yisrael is an experience rarely matched. Two of the rooms are dubbed the "Rebbe's Museum," that houses a selection of Judaica which the apartment owner has been accumulating since before he came on *aliyah* from Massachusetts in 1983. Pictures (mostly oil paintings) adorn virtually every inch of the walls, and more paintings and other artifacts clutter the floors, so that walking around is difficult. The bottom line is that the visitor is confronted by a constant barrage of religious messages, aided by Yisrael's insight and explanations.

The 150 or so paintings of famous rabbis "speak" clearly to the viewer. Each picture was hand-selected before it was purchased. These paintings are originals in which the artists have succeeded in conveying through minute detail the warmth and brilliance of their subjects. Some paintings have frames. Others do not. According to the "museum keeper," an elegant and eye-catching frame can detract from the painting. Material that does not fit into the two overcrowded rooms is being kept in rented storage space.

One painting has a special message. It depicts Roman soldiers wearing helmets and sacrificing a large coin on the altar, presumably of the defiled Second Temple. In the corner is Moses carrying the Ten Commandments and pointing to the altar. The artist's intention is to show that the Torah represents a spiritual goal that negates the wealth-oriented materialism of the Romans.

Modern photographs comprise about five percent of the material, highlighted by a picture of Rabbi Moshe Sternbuch of the *Eida*, with whom the museum owner is particularly close.

Not all in the Rebbe's Museum is paintings. There is a massive six-foot-tall Elijah's Chair for circumcisions that was constructed in Austria and requires several people to lift; the chair has extensive wooden engravings. Another unique item is a large brass sink that originated in a synagogue in Syria and is designed for washing one's hands. There is also a bust of Moses housed in a case to protect what Mr. Yisrael says is pure silver.

Some one hundred coverings for Torah scrolls, many of which are antique, are owned by the museum. Some were bought, and others were salvaged from genizah. Most are hand-made.

The Rebbe's Museum is on the second floor of Rechov Yeshayahu 11 in Jerusalem. It is open twenty-four hours a day with prior arrangement (Tel. 02-590 2657, 052-861 2668). A NIS 10 entrance fee is requested.

Religious Zionist Archives

These archives can be of interest if you are interested in researching aspects of the Mizrachi movement or religious Zionist history in Israel or abroad. Prior appointment is necessary, since hours are irregular and staff is limited.

The archives are located in the building of Mossad Rabbi Kook, founded by Rabbi Yehudah Leib (Fishman) Maimon (1875–1962) in 1937, just off Shderot Herzl. This collecton should not be confused with the Central Zionist Archives next to the Israel Convention Center.

Rechov Rabbi Maimon 2. Hours by appointment; closed Friday–Shabbat. No fee. Tel. 02-652 6231.

Rockefeller Museum

Visiting the Rockefeller Museum opposite the northeast corner of the Old City is to step back into history. The building was funded in major part by John D. Rockefeller (1839-1937), who donated two million dollars. Rockefeller stipulated that the building carry his name, but he died a year before the building was finished. Only after 1967 was the museum called "Rockefeller."

Other than the translation of exhibit descriptions into Hebrew, virtually nothing has changed in the museum since Jordanian days. In fact, little has changed since Mandate times. A sign carved into stone on the outside of the building still reads, "Government of Palestine." If the carved Hebrew lettering seems peculiar, most font designers agree. The letters date back to 1938, when the building was opened as the Palestine Archeology Museum. A Christian prelate with only a very minimal knowledge of Hebrew designed the font.

Today some of the Mandate signs are comical. The library, for example, is called *beit sefarim*, rather than the more modern *sifriyya*.

In October 1966 the Jordanians nationalized the museum. The museum was the site of a major battle during the Six Day War; pock marks from bullets can still be seen in the stone walls of the building. Since 1967 the museum has been run as part of the Israel Museum.

There are several items of definite Jewish interest in the museum. One series of exhibits, for example, illustrates Egyptian involvement in the Land of Israel during what were probably the last years of slavery in Egypt. It seems that the Egyptians sent a military expedition that reached at least as far north as Beit Shean. They were afraid of a local revolt instigated by the invasion of the "Sea People" (probably the Philistines) into the area. One Egyptian stele on display features Anat, the consort of the Canaanite Baal. This is only one of the indications that this specific idol worship permeated Egyptian culture.

Another exhibit features a collection of coins from the Bar Kochba period. The coins are well described, however in technical terminology. What is missing is the equation of these coins to the contemporary coinage mentioned in the Talmud.

What was the state of Jewish settlement in the Land of Israel after the Second Exile? To use modern terminology, the Romans adopted a policy of "population transfer," sending into exile the leaders of the Jewish community and much of the general population. It was assumed that the Jews who remained would assimilate into the new Roman population that was brought in to settle the land. As exhibits clearly show, the policy failed. Jews kept their identity. They even developed a new religious leadership.

A fourth century CE tomb memorial from Beit Shearim and written in Greek cites "Paregorios, the Rabbi." Overt Jews were accepted. The Rabbi's brother is mentioned as a civil servant. Their father was a member of the Goldsmiths' Guild.

There were synagogues as well. A decorated stone from Nabratein (near Tsefat) is on display; it is probably from a synagogue destroyed in the earthquake of 306 CE. There is a fourth century synagogue floor mosaic from Yafia (near Nazareth) and a fifth century Hebrew mosaic from Ussfiya (near Haifa). Jewish presence in the Land of Israel continued even after the destruction of the Second Temple. The exhibits in the museum prove that point most explicitly.

Egged buses 1 and 2 stop close to the Rockefeller Museum at Rechov Sultan Suleiman. Arrival by taxi or private car is recommended for those not familiar with the area. There is also a shuttle bus (free of charge) that operates two days a week from the Israel Museum (call 02-670 8811).

Hours: Sunday–Thursday, 1000–1700. Erev Shabbat/Holiday 1000–1400. Closed Shabbat. Entrance gratis. Tel. 02-628 2251.

Tips: Detailed guidebooks in English are available on loan at the desk, however they are very cumbersome to use, since some of the exhibits have been removed. There are tours sponsored by the Israel Museum.

The Israel Antiquities Authority occupies part of the building, and they are willing to provide guides when possible; call 02-620 4605.

Safra Square

During the 1930s the British Mandate Government built its administrative headquarters adjacent to the Russian Compound. The Jerusalem Municipality occupied a small building behind what was Barclay's Bank. The city had a small budget and made a deal with Barclay's—the bank financed construction in exchange for a thirty year bank lease on the southern part of the structure.

Almost adjacent to the mayor's office is Gan Daniel, a small park named after Daniel Auster (1893–1962), mayor from 1944–1945, and again from 1949–1950. During the Mandate, Gan Daniel was a center for transportation to Jaffa and other out-of-city destinations.

Over the years the municipal building became too small for the growing needs of the city. This was particularly true after 1967, when the city grew in area and population, as it absorbed the Arab population and attracted new residents. The municipal building of Jordanian Jerusalem was just off Jaffa Gate inside the Old City. It was too small to add significant space for the city's management.

The cornerstone for a new municipal complex, Safra Square (named after Jacob and Esther Safra, parents of Edmond J. Safra (1932-1999), a Jewish philanthropist) was laid in 1989. The new "city hall" was opened in 1993. This included a new main building and twelve auxiliary buildings, ten of which were renovations of historical structures. The primary architect was Abel Joseph Diamond (1932-), a South African who immigrated to Canada in 1964. Diamond also designed the Israel Foreign Ministry Building.

In the basement of the main building there is a miniature of central Jerusalem (used for planning purposes) and archives with an exhibit about Theodor "Teddy" Kollek (1911–2007), who served as mayor 1965–1993.

Tours of Safra Square are available in English and Hebrew on Mondays at 1000. Fee is NIS 10. Reservations at Tel. 02-629 5981.

Shaarei Zedek Hospital

The hospital traces its beginnings to 1873, when fundraising offices were opened in Frankfurt to solicit donations for a modern hospital to serve the needs of Jerusalem's Jewish residents. In 1894 the Ottoman government agreed to sell 2.5 acres of land for the hospital. Permits were slow. Architectural plans were drawn up, then construction commenced in 1896.

The construction supervisor for the hospital was Rabbi Yaacov Mann, a man with no prior building experience. His knowledge of Talmud and *Eruvin* helped him give extremely insightful comments on the building plans. On that basis he was appointed to oversee construction.

Even before the new building opened, Shaarei Zedek provided medical services. Dr. Moshe Wallach (1866–1957) arrived from Köln in the early 1890s and immediately started treating the sick in a make-shift clinic in the Old City. At night he made house calls. Dr. Wallach was to serve as head of Shaarei Zedek for half a century. He became a devoted student of Rabbi Yosef Chaim Sonnenfeld (1849–1932), and he was instrumental in making Shaaeri Zedek a religiously observant hospital in every sense of the phrase.

Finally, an opening date for the new hospital was selected—27 January 1902. Dignitaries assembled. The Ottoman ruler of Jerusalem was

**Shaarei Tzedek.
Building
the hospital on
Jaffa Road.
From
the exhibit
in the
new
hospital
lobby**

present. So were Ashkenazi Rabbi Shmuel Salant (1816–1909) and Sephardic Rabbi Haham Bashi Yaacov Shaul Eliashar. The timing was significant. It was the birthday of German Kaiser Wilhelm II, who holds a special place in the history of the hospital. A German government fund in his name gave money to the hospital until 1933, when the Nazis stopped the payments.

The hospital was very German in its orientation. Not only were its European offices in Frankfurt, its early records were kept in German. Dr. Wallach came from Germany; the legendary head nurse who joined the staff in 1916, Schwester Selma (1884–1984), trained in Hamburg, and preferred

German during her forty-eight year career since she never really learned Hebrew very well.

There were no ambulances weaving through the traffic of Jaffa Road guided by the blaring of a siren. The building was at the end of town, built amongst empty fields. The sick arrived by carriage, donkey and camel. At first there were twenty beds, but three years after opening funds were found to reach full capacity—sixty beds.

During World War I Shaarei Zedek was virtually a military hospital, treating Ottoman soldiers. A typhoid outbreak in 1916 strained the hospital's resources. As a concentration center for Ottoman soldiers, history was made on its grounds. There in the garden on 9 December 1917, Mayor Hussein Salim al-Husseini (died 1918) surrendered in the name of Ottoman forces to the Major-General John Stuart Mackenzie Shea (1869–1966), commander of the Sixtieth Division of the British Army. The scene was somewhat comical, as the well-dressed mayor ran from British soldier to British soldier (even sergeants), looking for someone to whom he might surrender.

There is a monument two blocks away in the park / traffic circle outside Otzar HaPoskim. The language on the memorial is exact—Ottoman surrender to the British took place near the spot.

In its early days the hospital had to worry about literally everything. During World War I there was a cow-shed where milk for the patients was taken from the cows. Wheat was planted in the garden, and it was used for Pesach *shmurah matzos* baked in the hospital. Dr. Wallach was a devout Jew, and year after year he erected his *sukkah* with salon, dining room, and bedroom (all carpeted, of course).

During the Six Day War the hospital suffered three direct hits during the fighting, but miraculously no one was hurt.

Over the years Shaarei Zedek has grown from its modest beginnings to a large facility opened in 1978 in the valley below Bayit Vegan. (The old building was renovated after years of neglect and is now used by the Israel Broadcasting Authority.)

Shaarei Zedek has steadfastly kept its strict Orthodox tradition. For many years Rabbi Eliezer Yehuda Waldenberg (1917–2006), author of the twenty-two volume Tzitz Eliezer, served as the unofficial but universally acclaimed rabbinic authority of the hospital. Rabbi Moshe Peleg is now responsible for *halachic* decisions, ranging from medical problems to administrative issues, particularly dealing with *Shabbat*.

There is an historical exhibit in the fourth floor ("entrance") lobby (next to the much smaller exhibit on medicine in Jerusalem). The lobby is open twenty-four hours.

Sheikh Badr and Emergency Cemeteries in 1948

There is a Jewish cemetery well hidden in the trees within two or three hundred meters of the Knesset and behind the Supreme Court building. The cemetery, Sheikh Badr, to this day called by the name of the Arab neighborhood that once stood there, is one of four or five emergency Jewish cemeteries established in 1948.

Fighting in Jerusalem started long before the Mandate was terminated in May 1948. The "Sambusky Cemetery" between Silwan and Mount Zion and stated in the seventeenth century could no longer be used after 1945. By March 1948 Jews could no longer access the Mount of Olives due to Arab attacks. The Mandate Government stopped Jews from going to the cemetery, theoretically because of safety. The last Jewish burial is exemplary of the situation. The British allowed burial of the five bodies collected during a week; burial was escorted by armed troops.

But, people continued to pass away. Some were killed in fighting. Others died from natural causes. Something had to be done to bury the dead.

A quick solution was the opening of an emergency cemetery, today called *Sanhedria*, across from the *Shmuel HaNavi* neighborhood at the beginning of the modern Ramot Road. There were, however, religious problems. The cemetery was controlled by the irreligious city committee, and it was feared that not everything regarding burial would be done according to religious law. A new solution had to be found for the religious community. (In later years the *Sanhedria* cemetery, on the Israeli side of no-man's land, became a permanent burial grounds under religious direction.)

The next burial grounds to be opened was about one hundred meters (325 feet) away in *Machanayim* on a field that later became a municipal sanitation garage after the dead were reburied elsewhere. The first funeral was two weeks after *Sanhedria* was opened. Some people, however, objected. Burial there was an affront. It was a blatant rejection of the emergency cemetery only meters away.

One possible solution was the open field next to Shaarei Zedek Hospital, then located on Jaffa Road.

The vacant land on the side of Shaarei Zedek belonged to the hospital, but Dr. Wallach strenuously objected to its use as a burial grounds. Wallach was certainly well-versed with the need for proper religious burial. Yet, he vigorously objected to burial on the unused land. The hospital was overcrowded with those wounded in the fighting. Dr. Wallach contended there was no room for a cemetery. Then, a moving event took place. A woman came to his office in tears and asked that her brother be buried on the plot of land. She contended that there was no option. That was the only place available. Wallach quickly changed his mind and allowed that burial, and as a consequence others afterwards. The woman and her deceased brother were children of Rabbi Yosef Chaim Sonnenfeld, Wallach's mentor.

Today several graves in the Shaarei Zedek cemetery are conspicuously empty. The deceased were reburied on the Mount of Olives after its capture in 1967.

The problem of religious burial continued. Shaarei Zedek could not be a long-term solution. The grounds were too small to accommodate large numbers. Another answer to the burial issue arose. Arabs had deserted the Sheikh Badr neighborhood. It was decided to open an emergency cemetery there, on a hill overlooking the southeastern part of Jerusalem. From the very beginning burial was stipulated to be temporary, allowing subsequent re-interment (*Yoreh De'a* 363). Generally, it is the family that stipulates temporary burial. In this case it was primarily the Burial Society, given war conditions and the Arab siege on Jerusalem. By the time the cemetery was closed, several hundred people had been buried there in two different sections, first in an upper area, then later in a lower area that had been previously used as a quarry. Eventually, a staircase was put in to connect the two burial zones.

Another cemetery was unique. On Shavuot 1948 tragedy struck. Rabbi Avraham Mordechai Alter (1866–1948), the Rebbe of Gur and author of *Imrei Emet*, passed away. The security situation in Jerusalem was precarious. He was buried in the courtyard of his house on Rechov S'fat Emet. (In later years one of his sons, the author of *P'nei Menachem*, was buried next to him.)

The year 1949 was pivotal in the history of burial in Jerusalem. It was then that the future of Sheikh Badr was decided upon. Long-terms planning would call for the Knesset and government buildings to move to one hill in the Sheikh Badr neighborhood. The campus of Hebrew University in the Israeli enclave on Mount Scopus could not be reached except by UN-escorted convoy once every two weeks; a new campus would be built on another hill of Sheikh Badr. The neighborhood would also be the site of the Israel Museum. The Sheikh Badr cemetery would be discontinued. It was closed, when the *Har HaMenuhot* cemetery was opened.

Soon the IDF realized there was also a need for a military cemetery in Jerusalem. The city was to be the capital of the new-born state. It was only appropriate that it contain burial grounds for the country's fallen soldiers. In the summer 1949 it was decided to consecrate a military cemetery on today's Mount Herzl. That burial ground was also reserved for non-military leaders of the Jewish State.

In 1948 it was hard to differentiate between civilian and soldier. Many Jews took up arms. Some Jews were reburied on Mount Herzl when that cemetery was opened. They fought against Arab attacks. They were killed, but in several cases the bodies were not identified. Or, the tombstones record all that is known–only a first name. But, the fallen are not forgotten.

The Sanhedria cemetery is accessible on busses 16, 28, 71, 72, 39. Machanayim has been redeveloped. The Shaarei Zedek and Sheikh Badr cemeteries can still be visited.

Shimon HaTzadik Grave

"By three things the world is sustained: Torah, Worship, and Deeds of Kindness." This familiar Mishnah from Ethics of the Fathers (1:2) is attributed to Shimon HaTzadik ben Yochanan, a member of the Great Assembly.

The grave of Shimon HaTzadik is in the Sheikh Jarrah neighborhood of East Jerusalem at the one end of the Kidron Valley. This is one of the many Roman-Byzantine era graves in a burial area that extended from the Valley and as far north as Ramat Eshkol and Sanhedria.

As tradition relates, several members of the Great Assembly were buried in a cave at the site. Today their names are no longer known, and the only surviving tradition is that concerning Shimon HaTzadik.

The area was always considered important to Jews, and in the 1880s a joint Ashkenazi-Sepharadi-Yemenite committee managed to raise sufficient funds to purchase the land. In 1891 *Nachalat Shimon* was founded for those Jews who wanted to live near the burial places. That neighborhood, however, was abandoned after the Arab riots of 1929.

The burial cave, itself, is closed. Prayer is in an adjoining room with a women's section and equipped for learning. There are daily public prayers (k'vatikin at sunrise) for those who want. Otherwise, there are laminated pages available with a prayer to be said, taken from *Sefer Sha'arei Dim'oh*.

Most popular times to visit the grave are Lag B'Omer, the Yahrzeit on 29 Tishrei, and for the first haircut of three-year-old boys.

Travel by taxi is recommended for those not familiar with the area, although Egged Bus No. 23 does stop reasonably close by.

For the record, there are other graves in the era. In the courtyard of the École Biblique (St. Étienne Church) at 6 Nablus Road there is a cave with graves and an ossuary purportedly dating to the period of the First Temple (about eighth century BCE based upon archeological estimation). As noted previously, a visit is not recommended.

There is also a grave in Ramat Eshkol that dates to the Byzantine Period and is not known to have any particular religious significance. The grave is known as "Eshkolot (cluster of grapes)," the design at the entrance to the burial cave. The name is coincidental. Ramat Eshkol was named for Levi Eshkol (1895–1969), the third prime minister of Israel.

Supreme Court *(See color plate 40, p. 110)*

Upon the declaration of the State of Israel, the Supreme Court was housed in the Russian Compound. It began to function in September, 1948 under the presidency of Chief Justice Moshe Smoira (1888–1961). In 1984, the Rothschild's donated a new building for the Supreme Court. Ram Karmi and his sister, Ada Karmi Melamed, of Tel Aviv won the architectural competition. The new Supreme Court building was dedicated on 10 November 1992.

The main functions of the Supreme Court are to hear requests for appeals of civil criminal cases, and to handle petitions against governmental authorities, prisoners' petitions and re-hearings of previous Supreme Court decisions. The public is allowed to attend all court proceedings except those held *in camera* and deal with security or matters protected by the right of privacy.

There are five courtrooms of various sizes for hearings. Each is designed in the spirit of a different ancient synagogue from the Talmudic period (200 CE–600 CE). Traditional themes dominate the architecture. The entrance to each courtroom recalls gates carved into a stone wall, reminiscent that in ancient times judges sat at the gates to the city.

The Supreme Court is at the head of a pyramid of secular courts. There is a parallel religious court system that operates strictly in accordance with Jewish Law in matters of personal status (marriage, divorce, etc.). The religious courts can also hear civil cases when both sides agree.

Rechov Sha'arei Mishpat. Open Sunday–Thursday, 0830–1430. Closed Shabbat. Tel. 02-675 9612. Hebrew tours lasting forty-five minutes at 1100. English tours at 1200.

Ticho House *(See color plate 41, p. 111)*

The Ticho House was built in the late nineteenth century by Rashid Nashishibi. Its early history, however, was problematic to say the very least. Five years after the house was built, it was sold to Moses Wilhelm Shapira (1830–1884), a memorable seller of antiquities (not to be confused with Moshe Shapira, who designed sun dials).

Shapira was born to Jewish parents in Kamenetsi, Poland (now in the Ukraine). Shapira's father had immigrated to Palestine, and in 1856 Moses Shapira followed accompanied by his grandfather, who died en route.

Upon arrival in Palestine, Shapira converted to Christianity and opened an antiquities shop on Christian Quarter Road. After the discovery of the Mesha Stele (named after Mesha, King of Moab) by F. A. Klein in Dibon, Jordan in 1868, there was intense interest in Biblical archeology and "Moabology." Klein, who was already successful selling ancient artifacts supplied to him by Rashid al-Kari, a local Arab, traveled to the Transjordan to find more artifacts. He managed to sell 1700 pieces to the museum in Berlin in 1873. With wealth came status. Shapira, prominent in the antiquities business, bought the large house and gardens from the Nashishibi family.

Then came Shapira's biggest find—fifteen fragments of the Book of Deuteronomy written on sheepskin in the seventh century BCE. He was on the verge of selling the fragments to the British Museum for £1,000,000, when the scam unfolded. The pieces sold to Berlin were forgeries. So were the Deuteronomy fragments. Shapira fled London in disgrace. He never returned home to Jerusalem. He traveled as far as Rotterdam, where he committed suicide.

Dr. Avraham Albert Ticho (1883–1960) and his wife, Anna (1894–1980), bought the house in 1924. The lower storey was the doctor's eye clinic and the upper floor became home to his wife's art collection. When Anna died in 1980, she bequeathed the house to the City of Jerusalem; it now belongs to the Israel Museum.

In the Ticho House there is a unique collection of ancient Chanukah menorahs. Originally there were some 150 items in the collection. After Dr. Ticho passed away in 1960, the collection was given to the now-disbanded Bezalael National Museum. Then the material was transferred to the Israel Museum, where some ten Chanukah lamps are on permanent display. Others, including an exquisite early twentieth century silver candelabrum from Germany and a sixteenth century brass Chanukah lamp from Italy, can be seen at the Ticho House.

Today the Ticho house is an off-site branch of the Israel Museum.

Rechov Rabbi Kook 7. Open Sunday, Monday, Wednesday, Thursday 1000–1700, Tuesday 1000–2200, Friday 1000–1400. Closed Shabbat. Tel. 02-624 5068.

There is an art library open Sunday, Monday, Wednesday, Thursday 1100–1800, Tuesday 1400–1800, Friday 1000–1200. A video about the life of Anna Ticho is screened upon request.Entry gratis. Closed Shabbat.

Third Wall *(See color plate 42, p. 111)*

Herod's building program showed every sign of megalomania in his quest for grandeur. One of his many projects was to grossly increase the size of Jerusalem by building what has become known as the Third Wall. The project was begun in 41 CE and quickly finished in 66 CE before the revolt. The wall was breached and virtually destroyed by the Romans in their quest to conquer Jerusalem.

A remaining segment of the Third Wall can be seen adjacent to the Paz gas station across from the American Consulate in East Jerusalem. This is also opposite the Museum on the Seam.

The route of the wall continued from there toward Mea Shearim. The street leading in that direction bears the name Third Wall (*Rechov HaHoma HaSh'lishit*). Recently another segment of the wall was discovered, when a pub near the Russian Compound was demolished for urban renewal; that section is not open to the public.

Time Elevator

This presentation on the entrance floor of Beit Agron in Jerusalem is an experiment in cinematography. Reminiscent of the Cinerama large multi-screen panoramic presentations of the 1950s and 1960s, the audience is brought to feel every movement in a time tunnel. The sensations are augmented by chairs that vibrate and tremble.

The technique is used to accompany a thirty minute overview of the history of Jerusalem. The technique is very successful, particularly for children. The message, however, is poor; the script of the film and its production are problematic.

The first segments of the film deal with the Binding of Isaac, King Solomon, and Jeremiah. There are inaccuracies, but the general approach is interesting—to give a human approach to verses by having scenes acted out.

Another positive technique is showing typical Greek artistic freezes, then animating them to stress their reality and better illustrate the activities they depict.

The author of the script raised several substantive issues. In one scene a boy is restrained by his parents as he tries to act openly against the Roman occupation. Yes, there were those who joined the Jewish Revolt and others who quietly sided with it but remained silent. Then the son joins the Revolt, is caught, and crucified (the most common means of Roman capital punishment during this period).

The handling of the rise of Christianity is objectionable. Skipping centuries, Helen is shown as a figure traveling about, identifying historical sites, spreading Constantine's edit of the new state religion, and supervising the destruction of idols. The actor playing the would-be member of the Jewish

Revolt is re-cast with a cross dangling from his neck, tacitly implying that he had converted. The play-up to coy a Christian audience is obvious and out of place.

As centuries go by, the Madaba map is mentioned, the rise of Islam is recalled, and a quick mention is made of the Crusader and subsequent Mamluk periods. In gigantic leaps Israeli independence is stressed, then significant treatment is given to the Six Day War. It is at least encouraging to listen to the reactions of the soldiers who conquered the Western Wall—even for the non-religious the Western Wall [and the Temple] are still major aspects of our faith.

The movie concludes with glimpses of Jerusalem. On one point the script writer is absolutely correct—Jerusalem is a beautiful city. Jerusalem is certainly worth seeing, but this movie is not! Better use can be found for the steep entrance fee. The cinema-graphic technique is also very strong and holds good potential to both teach and entertain. It is a shame that the technique was not used with a better and more appropriate script.

Beit Agron, Rechov Hillel 37. Open Sunday–Thursday 1000–1700, Friday 1000–1400. Not Shomer Shabbat. Entry NIS 50. Tel. 02-624 8381. Extended hours during holiday periods. Children under five not admitted.

Tomb of the Kings *(See color plate 43, p. 111)*

This first century tomb, used by the family of Queen Helene of Adiabene, is Jerusalem's largest grave of the period. Flavius Josephus writes that the Queen converted to Judaism in the first century CE and came to live in Jerusalem. The name of the tomb, "Kings," is derived from the mistaken nineteenth century supposition that the magnificent tomb was used for burial by the House of David.

The tomb was a marvel in its day. An ancient description relates that the nine meter (thirty feet) wide staircase led to a series of ritual baths in front of the twenty-eight meter (ninety-two foot) façade, where water drained from carved tunnels.

Theft from graves and vandalism were common, so the architect took care to complicate entry by devising a series of "secret" actions (moving a large stone, which then moved weights) to allow access. Despite this intricate arrangement, there is evidence that the tombs were looted over the centuries.

As to burial, the tomb contains eight chambers with both burial niches and stone sarcophagi (now in the Louvre in Paris). Bodies were wrapped and left to decompose. The bones were letter interred in the niches or in the sarcophagi, presumably after a year had passed.

The Tomb of the Kings is currently closed to visitors, except upon special arrangement.

Yad Ben Zvi *(See color plate 44, p. 112)*

Yitzchak Ben Zvi (1884–1963) left a legacy of achievement. He served as Israel's second president, from the death of his predecessor, Chaim Weizmann (1874–1952) until his own passing during his third term. Ben Zvi was a scholar, carefully documenting distant communities and the historiography of Eretz Yisrael. It is only fitting that in 1971 Yad Ben Zvi was established to further knowledge in these two areas.

Ben Zvi was a traveler at heart, seeking first-hand information about Jews in far-off and unusual lands. Born in Galicia, his personal orientation was Western; so, "unusual" meant Sephardic. Before World War I, he investigated Sephardic communities in Izmir, Constantinople, and Salonika. In later years he visited Jews in Beirut and Damascus. Subsequently, he even spent time in Aden, looking into Yemenite Jewish traditions. Wherever and whenever possible, Ben Zvi collected documentation. Those papers and books became the basis of the Yad Ben Zvi Library, today quietly tucked away in the first and second floors of a residential building in Jerusalem's Rechavia neighborhood.

Jerusalem does not lack Judaica libraries, but the collection at Yad Ben Zvi is special. There are, for example, over 3000 Sephardic manuscripts, most never published and many not available elsewhere even on microfilm. These handwritten documents range from eighteenth century Libyan marriage registers to otherwise unknown liturgical poetry, to early twentieth century community papers from the Balkans. There are also over 30,000 pictures in the Photo Archives, including the collection of Ze'ev Vilnai, the famed historiographer and author of numerous volumes about the Land of Israel.

Documentation about Sephardic communities is extensive, whether talking about the books they have produced or external studies about them. Some items are curiosity pieces, such as a Jewish Bible in the Maharas language of India or a Hebrew Primer from Calcutta. Many materials in the collection have direct research value, such as synagogue leaflets and histories.

Not everything is from an exotic location. There are publications from the Sephardic communities of New York and London. Although other libraries have collections of similar materials, in collecting such ephemera (items not printed by regular publishers) no institution has "everything."

A distinct advantage of Yad Ben Zvi is that most material is open-shelf, according to location to facilitate the locating of desired publications and allow convenient hands-on search.

Scholars will find unique items in Yad Ben Zvi. There is a copy of the first printing of the Zohar from 1550. There are also numerous Sephardic responsa volumes and sermons, many in manuscript form or long out of print.

The other overall topic of the Yad Ben Zvi Library is the history of the Land of Israel. Again, the collection is open-shelf and catalogued according to geographic location. There is considerable material about Jerusalem and its neighborhoods.

Yad Ben Zvi is more than a library. They also publish books, which sell both in-house and through regular commercial outlets; and, they offer a wide-ranging education program, running from lectures to courses, often including tours (sometimes in English). The program features ancient topics such as Jerusalem before the destruction of the Second Temple, and more modern subjects such as the settlement of the Nachlaot and Rechavia neighborhoods. Particularly for repeat visitors to Israel who have seen basic sites, these tours (or privately arranged tours) are a practical method to broaden understanding.

Nothing is static. The library is in the tedious process of computerizing all their material with the goal of being available online. Another current project is the microfilming of Ladino newspapers which have become brittle with the passage of time and are now crumbling. The biggest project is underfoot to transfer the library and education departments to a nearby building now being rennovated.

Not far away, at Rechov Alfasi 10, is a Second Temple era burial area, known as the Tomb of Jason, based on an inscription citing that name.

The Yad Ben Zvi Library is at Rechov Ibn Ezra No. 13, First Floor. Open Sunday–Thursday 0900–1700. Closed Friday–Shabbat. Tel. 02-539 8811.

Yad Sarah

Charity is a cherished Jewish value, and Yad Sarah stands out as one of the foremost Israeli institutions providing assistance to the needy, in this case the handicapped. The organization, founded in 1978, has 103 offices run by a small core staff and more than six thousand volunteers.

Yad Sarah's best-known service is the lending of medical and rehabilitative equipment on a short-term basis free of charge to anyone who needs it. They have over 250,000 items, from crutches and wheelchairs to oxygen concentrators and electronic monitors.

The tour of the Yad Sarah House is an eye-opener as to the equipment and assistance available to the handicapped. The synagogue on the seventh floor provides an excellent view of southern Jerusalem.

In conjunction with Hadassah, Yad Sarah runs a professional library with literature about numerous disabilities and debilitating diseases. It is possible to sit down and read books and journals, however the primary purpose of the library is to receive medical questions and supply answers at no charge. (Names of doctors and clinics are not provided.) Most of the staff speaks English as well as Hebrew. Questions can be asked by telephone (02-644 4500) or in person.

Yad Sarah House, 124 Herzl Boulevard. Tours lasting up to one hour are available in English on Sundays and Tuesdays at 1000. There is no fee, and the tour is wheelchair accessible. Building closed Friday–Shabbat.

Yad VaShem

Warsaw, April 1943. It was a very different Pesach. On 18 January German soldiers had tried to deport Jews from the Warsaw ghetto to extermination camps, but four days of resistance put an end to Nazi efforts. This time, on 19 April as Jews were making last preparations for the Pesach seder, German soldiers entered the ghetto to start deportations. The heroic resistance that ensued would last until 8 May, when the partisans' main bunker was overtaken. The ghetto fell, but a legend of courage and bravery was born. That story of the few defending themselves against the many is only one of the dozens of episodes described in the exhibits on display at Yad VaShem, the most renowned of the three public Holocaust museums in Israel.

Most tourists wander through the museum, looking at pictures retelling the rise of Hitler and the horrors of his regime. The Biblical Amalek must never be forgotten, but the display is not the most interesting aspect of a visit to Yad VaShem. The forty-five acre complex houses a treasure of information that is available without charge—not only in the museum.

On 19 September 1941 Heinz Jöst, a driver in the German army, entered the Warsaw Ghetto and took 129 photographs of everyday life. Only several of the photographs are on display in the museum. The rest, however, can be found in the library archives located in a separate building.

Almost 115,000 books are in the library whose staff is also a rerference point for items ranging from several thousand periodicals to numerous exhibits not on public display. There are 160,000 photographs and thousands of videocassettes. Several years ago this author queried the library about document forgeries used by underground forces. Staff found pages in books, unpublished recollections of partisan fighters, and a "kit" used to issue false identity cards in Occupied France.

The Hall of Names is an interesting project. We all jokingly complain of being a number, not a person, when we are asked to write down our driver's license or passport numbers. The Hall of Names is a serious project since 1953. The six million who perished were people, not numbers. Each had a name. This is a list of those victims—their names, parents, residence, and details of their deaths. The list has been computerized and is on-line. Not only is it worthwhile to check the list for information about family murdered by the Nazis; it is equally meaningful to fill out a page about those who died under Nazi rule so that others can benefit from the details. This author, for example, found a report with new information about family members who perished.

Not everything at Yad VaShem is academic. The Children's Memorial, designed by Moshe Safdie and opened in 1988, is an emotionally moving monument to a million and a half youngsters whose lives were cut short so tragically. The theme is the stars of the heavens, too numerous to be counted. Through techniques of mirrors five candles produce thousands of lights, too numerous to be counted.

The museum is new. It replaces the dry presentation of previous years by using extensive audio-visual testimonies and numerous artifacts from the Holocaust. The new museum took ten years to plan and build. It is absolutely worthwhile. Visits take between ninety minutes and three hours.

Yad VaShem can be reached by bus to Mt. Herzl, then a five-minute walk or a shuttle bus. Hours for the museum Sunday–Wednesday, 0900–1700; Thursday 0900–2000, Friday and eves of holidays 0900–1400. Closed Shabbat. Library hours: 0830–1700 Sunday–Thursday. Last orders for books in the closed stacks is 1500.

Tours (English and Hebrew) daily at 1100 for a NIS 30 fee or by audio tape (for a fee) in seven languages. No fees for regular museum visit or library, but there is a charge for parking.

Yad VaShem is theoretically accessible for the handicapped, but there is some rough pavement that makes passage difficult. There are handicapped parking spaces and bathrooms.

Yemin Moshe

During the first centuries of Ottoman rule Jerusalem was a small and quiet city restricted to the walls rebuilt by Suleiman. The few tourists who came left no real mark. Perhaps tourist is the wrong word. It has the connotations of groups following a guide and being taken from place to place.

At this time there were no tour guides. There were no groups. There were travelers, out to rediscover sites know from earlier literature and to pray at holy sites. One could well say that the ventures to the Holy Land were a sequel to the general European rediscovery of the classical world.

In the mid-nineteenth century this pattern changed. For various reasons there was a new European interest in the Holy Land. European powers opened offices there and stood behind the expansion of cities. Jerusalem grew. It is against this background that Moshe Montefiore stood behind the building in the late 1850s of the first Jewish neighborhood outside the walls of the Old City—Yemin Moshe (named, of course, after Moshe Montefiore). His dream was to enable Jews—Sephardim and Ashkenazim—to live together and build a modern city. Almost concurrently, Moslems also established housing outside the city walls.

Yemin Moshe, symbolized by its windmill (built in Canterbury, England and brought to Jerusalem in 1857 to grind flour for the poor), was a failure. Fear of bandits convinced many that it was not safe to live outside the city walls. The attractively priced housing of Yemin Moshe was insufficient to induce people to move in. Finally, financial inducements were offered to attract residents.

Just prior to the end of the Palestine Mandate the last British Governor of Palestine noticed that the Haganah had constructed an outpost atop the roof of the windmill. He quickly dispatched three explosive experts to blow up the windmill. Outside the windmill the three noticed a small sign relating that it had been constructed by an English nobleman from Ramsgate, a seaside town on the Isle of Thanet. Ironically, the demolition experts were from Ramsgate! They refused to carry out orders. They agreed to explode only the dome of the building. After the end of the Mandate the outpost was rebuilt.

Over the years Yemin Moshe, offering a magnificent view of the Old City walls but built on a steep slope, became run-down. Proximity to Mandate military headquarters in the King David, encirclement during the War of Independence, then anxiety about Jordanian sniper fire, all did not help. In recent years the area has been totally renovated with landscaped parks and upscale housing. Yemin Moshe has also become a center for artists and art galleries.

There is one rather different site bordering Yemin Moshe. Cut into a poorly marked hill and fenced off to prevent damage is a burial cave in which members of the family of Herod are buried.

Moshe Montefiore visited the Holy Land seven times from 1827 until 1875. From 1834 he traveled in his own private horse-drawn coach, which was restored and put on display in 1967. In 1986, however, that coach was destroyed by fire. Four years later the remaining slivers of wood were refashioned into a rebuilt coach, which can now be seen behind protective glass opposite the windmill.

The Moses Montefiore Museum is in the windmill. Hours are posted as Sunday–Thursday 0900–1600 and Friday 0900–1300, closed Shabbat, but do not be fooled by the sign. The museum is closed, and there is no indication when it will reopen.

Zichron Moshe *(See color plate 45, p. 112)*

This neighborhood, named for Moshe Montefiore and bought with monies from a fund in his name, was officially started in 1905, but building had already commenced the previous year.

Originally, Zichron Moshe, designed with wide streets, detached houses, and gardens, was designated as a neighborhood for prosperous residents. A key factor was the already existent Lamel School (featured on a 2005 Israel postage stamp) on Rechov Yishayahu, boasting an enrollment of upper class children. The Edison Theater, built in 1932 and demolished in 2005, stood across the street. True to the flavor of the Mandate-era neighborhood, the theater hosted performances of the philharmonic orchestra amongst other events.

Today the most famous site is the Zichron Moshe Synagogue, a building with a main synagogue and several smaller rooms for other minyanim. Every day there is an almost non-stop series of Daf Yomi classes in Hebrew, Yiddish, and English.

Zion Square

The original development of West Jerusalem was centered on a triangle of streets comprising King George, Ben Yehudah, and Jaffa. Zion Square is at the intersection of the latter two streets.

During Mandate times Zion Square was best known for the 22 February 1948 bombing under the direction of Hajj Al-Amin Al-Husseini (1895–1974), that left 52 people dead and 123 wounded.

Today Rechov Ben Yehudah has been turned into a pedestrian mall emphasizing tourist stores, and Zion Square is a center for informal secular youth gatherings. There are numerous pubs and restaurants in Nachalat Shiva, just off the Square.

Index of Jerusalem Place Names